ACKNOWLEDGEMENTS

I would like to thank Peter McGregor for his suggestion that my original report to the Trustees of the Anglo-German Foundation should be re-written in book form, and for the help and support he has given me. I am also grateful to Hans Wiener for the many helpful suggestions he made on the form the report should take, and Walter Segal and Robert Clayton for supplying detailed information and drawings of the projects.

I am indebted to John and Bertha Turner for reading the draft and giving me so much of their time for corrections and suggestions. However, responsibility for the style and content of the final work is entirely mine.

I am grateful for the help and advice given by many friends and colleagues, both in the writing of the report and in the work leading to it. Among these I would especially mention Stan Windass, Bill Edwards, Andrew Hake, Ken Hislop, Bill Carlton, Paul Jacques, David Pritchard, Michael Drake, Jean Stead and Mary Corfield.

Peter Stead
September 1978

SHORT GLOSSARY OF TERMS

ACT A decree passed by a legislative body i.e. Parliament.

BUILDING REGULATIONS
These are rules authorised by Parliament which govern how detailed work in all buildings is undertaken. All plans for house improvement must usually meet these regulations, and Councils employ Building Inspectors to enforce them.

CIRCULAR
Recommendations and guidelines from central government to local councils — not statutory.

DOE
The Department of the Environment; a central Government department, full of civil servants, some researching and trying their best to influence government policy, others attempting to administer those policies. Deals with all environmental matters, plus housing, planning, transport, building construction, etc.

HOUSING ASSOCIATIONS
Non-profit making organisations which rent houses, usually to families 'in need'. Run by groups of people, often professionals, who are directly accountable to the Housing Corporation.

HOUSING CO-OPERATIVE
A type of Housing Association, where the tenants are also the landlords. Non-profit making, getting its money from the Housing Corporation.

HOUSING CORPORATION
A Government body set up to supervise the Housing Association movement; effectively part of the DOE. Issues guidance to Associations and keeps an eye on their activities.

OPTION-MORTGAGE
A Mortgage, either from a Building Society or Local Authority where you pay a lower rate of interest, but don't get tax relief. Can be cheaper than an ordinary mortgage for low income families.

PARKER MORRIS STANDARD
A standard for house building first introduced in 1961. Local Authorities are required to build to these standards, but new private dwellings normally

SELF-BUILD HOUSING GROUPS AND CO-OPERATIVES

Ideas in Practice

A Report by Peter Stead

The Anglo-German Foundation for the Study of Industrial Society was established by an inter-governmental agreement between the Federal Republic of Germany and the United Kingdom following a generous initiative of the German Federal Government which was given expression during a state visit to Britain of the then Federal President, the late H. E. Dr. Gustav Heinemann. It was incorporated by a Royal Charter granted on the 5th December 1973 The Patrons of the Foundation are H. R. H. The Prince Philip, Duke of Edinburgh, and H. E. Herr Walter Scheel, President of the Federal Republic of Germany.

Financial support for the Foundation is now provided by both Governments, which each appoint six Members to the Board of Trustees.

The Foundation initiates and supports the study of the social, economic and political problems of Western industrial society, drawing particularly on the resources of the two countries in tackling common problems. A major part of the programme is concerned with the dissemination by publication, conferences or seminars of the results of such studies.

The opinions expressed in this report are entirely those of the author.

ISBN 0 905492 19 6   £3.50   Ref: 0026

fall below it. The standard refers to a house's internal space, heating and general design.

SELF-BUILD SOCIETY

A group of not less than seven people who form a limited liability company to build their houses together using their own labour. When the houses are completed they are sold to the individual members and the group is then wound-up.

CONTENTS

Introduction

"Is housing an object merely for consumption and/or investment, and is owner-building just another means to attain those ends? No one can give a simple answer to that question; yet our research suggests that a man who builds his house gains something more than shelter and equity. If this is true, it should be encouraged because it represents the basic human desire to exercise control over the making of one's environment — which may be especially important both to those who have relatively few economic options in life and to those who wish greater personal fulfilment".

William C. Grindley

INTRODUCTION

This report is about self-help and co-operative housing experience in England at present. Although highly particular in relation to worldwide experience, the English cases throw further light on general issues and what increasingly appear to be universal principles of local development. To introduce Peter Stead's invaluable contribution, an account of current procedures and of illustrative cases, I speak from my experience in the New World of North and South America where I have spent two-thirds of my working life advising on housing policy for low income people, and in this, my native country to which I returned a few years ago.

Peter Stead is of the 4th generation from a family of Yorkshire builders. He is also a teacher with wide experience both in the United States and as Head of the Department of Construction of Huddersfield Technical College — a post he gave up in order to do what he describes in this report. He also knows something of the Third World at first hand, from his service in Asia; and is therefore singularly well qualified to take action in a direct relationship with people struggling to house themselves to their own satisfaction in self-reliant ways. It is a continuing source of deep satisfaction for myself that Peter has committed himself to putting the ideas published in Freedom to Build into practise. I am proud to be associated with him.

We are now working together following up proposals for a long-term programme of action research and development, which we presented together in the HABITAT Forum at the U.N. Conference on Human Settlements at Vancouver in the Summer of 1976. These are summarised in my book 'Housing by People'.

There is no better way of understanding why things are not working out and what can and should be done in our field than by getting into it. Necessarily, the brief for this report is to describe that experience and to point out where it is leading.

The cases reported bear the same stamp of bureaucrat centralism that I observed and experienced in Latin America, and which Bertha Turner and our North American colleagues and I observed together throughout the United States. In those countries there are astonishing differences between the tiny proportion of houses produced by centrally sponsored, self-help housing projects and programmes and the huge amount of locally self-determined, self-help housing produced (with some institutional support in the U.S.A. but generally without in Latin America). These may not be paralleled in the United Kingdom or in modern Europe, but the few cases of self-reliant (and institutionally supported) self-help housing that we have seen at first hand in this country suggest constraints and potentials.

The central issue raised by Peter Stead's report is the same as that raised by the American experiences in both North and South alike. Can socially viable housing be economically supplied by ever-larger corporate organisations? If the answer is 'No, hardly at all in low-income countries and only temporarily in rich countries' then the potential for self-reliant, self-help and co-operative action is vital. Obviously in poor countries and increasingly in rich countries, an adequate and just production and distribution of housing depends upon the responsible participation of housing users — as self-managers caring for their own homes in the first place and, for those both able and willing, as self-builders as well.

The practical issues are illustrated by Peter Stead's case histories and face all concerned, both in the United Kingdom and elsewhere. They cluster around the relationships between people and their government. We in the United Kingdom are more fortunate than most in that the British people and their governments are on comparatively good terms. The suggestion that they can, should and sometimes actually *do* work together at local levels is neither absurd nor subversive. The experience described in this report does suggest that common assumptions and expectations on both the demand and the supply side of housing in Britain lead people and organisations inevitably down the well-trodden path toward the bureaucratic trap. The common assumption that local housing needs are 'things' that can only be supplied through centrally administered projects and programmes is perhaps more deeply ingrained here, where it has the longest history, than anywhere else. The alternatives to these 'categorical programmes' of corporately pre-determined goods and services for corporately defined categories of people are difficult to visualise in our British context. The idea of networks of suppliers and open institutions providing for and supporting self-reliant actions by people and of small organisations at the local level is alien and hard for many to see. Yet some people with enough money can and do use the networks and institutions still open to the comfortably well-off for building their own houses. Occasionally these networks are even used by people with moderate incomes, if they find the right methods. Here in Britain it seems likely that the contrasts between sponsored programmes of self-help housing and autonomous 'owner-built' housing in the U.S.A. or squatter-built housing in Third World countries, is presently finding its expression in the management, maintenance and improvement of existing stock rather than in the demand for new housing. A very large amount of home-improvement does go on, proven by the huge and expanding market for Do-it-Yourself supplies, and the rather low take-up of improvement grants by individual households and non-commercial groups. This activity is likely to show the same proportions of successes and savings as those described for new housing in other and newer countries. In the more limited field of upgrading one's own home, there are fewer mysteries and complications involving mortgage borrowing, planning permission and the obligatory hire of specialist contractors. As I have just proven for myself, anyone with a little knowledge of simple skills and the will to learn by doing, can enormously increase what one gets for the money spent on home improvements by doing them oneself. As everyone who does knows, it is relatively easy and straightforward, as long as one gets the tools and materials, and specialist advice or assistance when needed, at prices one can afford or within the budget of what one's local bank manager is prepared to advance. Most banks will lend for home improvements without half the complications of a local government grant which often proves more expensive as well.

The extension of networks of supplies and supporting institutions providing above all, land and credit for new construction is constrained by the barriers that Peter Stead identifies. As he points out, these are mainly social and institutional. There are few areas outside central business districts of major towns and cities which do not have usable land in small plots or occupied by empty structures which self-help and co-operating groups could use. With current income levels and available subsidies, there are few able and willing potential self-helpers unable to afford the financial costs or the spare time required and there is a plentiful supply of suitable tools and materials. As the Downsview and Toothill self-build cases so clearly show, the barriers are the generally well-meaning institutions on which people depend for access to the available resources. While it is necessary to be accountable for public funds, a means of getting more value for money is not being recognised and fostered. The barriers are erected mainly by the welding of many necessary and normally independent operations together with many others not so necessary, into standardised amalgams of exceedingly complex and rigid procedures. These are well illustrated by the cases presented and painstakingly documented in the last three chapters.

It must be clear to any unbiased reader, as it is to all who have been through experiences of the kinds described, that major changes must be made before the evident potential of self-help and co-operative action can be realised. The task is to build up and extend the networks supplying and the institutions providing access to basic resources and infrastructures that self-governing households and groups must have in order to use their own resources. These must eventually replace the categorical programmes and rigidly interconnected procedures currently required. The questions put by Peter Stead's cases, analyses and commentary are: to what extent can these norms be circumvented? To what extent can they be used in ways that change them? What would an alternative structure look like in the British context? And how can it be achieved?

Peter Stead does not attempt to answer these questions in his report. Our experience so far is only enough to ask the questions. Recommendations at this stage can only be suggestions for action research, to accelerate the process of learning by doing.

John F. C. Turner.

London
August 1978

PREFACE

1. HISTORICAL BACKGROUND

This report is based upon my practical experience of working in the self-help housing field over the last twenty years. In the early years my work was mostly experimental, building a series of houses to test how people might build their homes in the quickest and easiest way. I used simple designs and light, easily assembled components which required the minimum of building skills, and I tried to listen to what people required and what their aspirations were. I think I had only a limited success, probably because I was concentrating too much on the technical aspects of what I was doing. Then in 1974, whilst I was studying at the Architectural Association Graduate School, I was fortunate enough to meet and learn from John F. C. Turner;[1] of the ways in which groups of people could begin to think seriously of actually designing and constructing, or managing, their housing, and using the resources available to them to increase their control over their environment.

Very soon after this, a chance came to put some of this learning into practice when the Anglo-German Foundation agreed to fund a proposal by Alternative Society[2] to set up the Centre for Alternatives in Urban Development in a disused farmhouse on the outskirts of Swindon. It was to be a resource centre whose purpose was to foster a radically different kind of urban growth, both in the neighbouring borough of Thamesdown and elsewhere, a healthy growth by real community participation in planning and building and energy economy, local productive enterprises, and the good use of the land for food production. A daunting task at that time, but at least we had some local support, even from a few Thamesdown councillors and officers. In December 1974 we secured a lease on the farmhouse and formed an executive committee of local people and Alternative Society members to run the centre. I was appointed Building Consultant and my task was to:

— Establish a service offering free and independent technical, legal and management advice to people who wished to start self-help housing projects;

— Start discussions with the Borough of Thamesdown on how we might start some pilot projects together, using self-build and co-operative methods;

— Encourage all the people interested to use the Centre as a place where they could meet together and discuss how these schemes might be put into practice.

I hope this report gives a fair picture of the outcome of the work we have done from the Centre in the last three years. Part I tells the story of the Swindon case studies and concludes with some questions and suggestions. Part II is in manual form to document in more detail the points touched upon

1

in the case studies. Since writing this part of the report the Co-operative Housing Agency has been closed down and its functions taken over by the Housing Corporation, so all references to the Agency now apply to the Housing Corporation and its regional offices. The whole is addressed to people who find themselves in the same position as those in the case studies, and to local government councillors and officers who may want to follow the example of Thamesdown and help people to find alternative ways of solving their housing needs. Although the report is about new buildings, I hope many of the lessons learned can be applied by those who are trying so hard to deal with the problems of rehabilitating existing housing stock in the cities, and that they will not be too critical that I have so restricted the content.

LESSONS FROM EXPERIENCE

2. THREE CASE STUDIES IN SWINDON

The first iniative taken by the Centre for Alternatives in Urban Development was a Summer School for the people of Swindon (Borough of Thamesdown) entitled 'Alternatives in Housing'.[3] In 1975 the Borough suffered as much as most communities in England from a scarcity of houses and local facilities as well as from high and rising costs. It was more fortunate than most, however, as it had many different industries and employment opportunities; it was a designated expanding town[4] and had a forward looking Council actively searching for better ways of getting things done. So that when the idea of a summer school, based on the theme of 'more homes and community facilities for less money', was discussed with members and officers of the Council as well as organised community groups there was general agreement to support it.

We arranged a two week programme, in September of 1975, to deal with the following questions:

— Can residents, whether owner occupiers, or tenants of privately or publicly owned houses, get better and cheaper services through associations and co-operative action?
— Can people actually build their own homes or community facilities, well and economically, either as individual households or co-operatively?
— Are industrialised building systems really cheaper, either to build or to use and maintain?
— Are there any other ways of using modern tools and materials that reduce building or running costs?
— Can small builders and specialist contractors successfully compete with larger firms for quality or quantity?

and the answers to these and other vital questions were discussed in the light of experience with actual buildings and improvements successfully carried out in England by a number of invited practitioners[5] who had been responsible for the examples used in the opening lectures.

There were sixty-six registered participants, including officers and members of the local authority and members of local community groups, and the outcome was a better understanding of the possible practical answers to these questions by those present. But equally important was the understanding and goodwill we established with the members and officers of the Borough which led to their active support of the projects described in the following chapters.[6]

3

The three case studies show people who are in many ways typical of groups throughout Britain who are struggling to find the ways and means to build the kind of houses they want. The Downsview and Toothill self-builders were in the low to medium income scale, in unsatisfactory public or private rented houses in most cases, with little or no chance of qualifying for a mortgage large enough to buy the houses being sold in Thamesdown. They wanted good-sized family houses in pleasant surroundings and, over a period of time, realised that the only way to achieve this was to build for themselves.

The Toothill co-operative was formed because we had established that there was an urgent need for more single-person accommodation in Thamesdown. In the early 1970's a number of large companies had moved into Swindon because of its proximity to the newly completed M4 motorway, and many of their employees were single people. The intake at the local Technical College was increasing, mostly by the addition of 3 year resident students from outside the town, and the problem of how to house them was becoming acute. The regional hospital in Swindon was also expanding its student nursing facilities, and again this was causing problems of single-person housing which the health authorities had no resources to deal with.

At the same time, the Borough was demolishing houses in the centre of the town to make way for a regional shopping and commercial centre, many of which had been providing rented space particularly for students. Yet there was little or no provision for single people in most of the Borough's new housing schemes.

So the idea of a co-operative, to take care of at least a part of this urgent need, received not only the support of single people but also the employers and institutions concerned.

The Borough had acquired large tracts of farmland which it was developing for housing in what is known as the "western expansion" of Swindon, and it was here that sites were made available for the two Toothill schemes. Toothill being the name of the area of the first part of this expansion. The site allocated to the Downsview group was in the southern part of the town in an area known as the Dorcan; an area of new housing, with good views towards the Marlborough downs, which the Borough had been developing since 1971 and which was almost completed.

So we were fortunate to have not only a local authority who supported our ideas but one which had land readily available. However, even though our potential owner-builders were able to overcome this first hurdle relatively easily, there were many more difficult ones to come, as the case studies will show.

4

3.　DOWNSVIEW SELF-BUILD HOUSING ASSOCIATION LTD.

In its Circular[7] following the Housing Act of 1974, the Government declared that it was anxious that help and encouragement should be given to those who were prepared to contribute by their own physical efforts to the solution of their housing problems, and who could thus make available additional resources to help meet general housing needs. Although self-build schemes were not envisioned to be spreading on a really wide scale, the Government believed they could nevertheless play a more important role in the future, and sought to provide the means for an increasing number of people to take advantage of self-build as an answer to their housing problems.

The people who met together in Wootten Basset near Swindon in November 1974 certainly saw self-build as the only way to get a house of their own. An article in the local newspaper at that time, under the heading "Mike aims to build his dream in bricks and mortar" described how Council tenant Mike Lundberg's dream of having a house of his own was brought nearer to realisation when he decided to build it himself. He had advertised in the newspaper the previous month for people who would be willing to form a self-build group, and the response came from sixteen men, amongst whom were plumbers, carpenters and electricians, all keen to build their own houses.

Most of them lived in Council houses, some in caravans, and two already owned their houses but were not satisfied with either their size or quality. Fifteen were married with one or more children, one was married with no children, and their average age was just over thirty years.

On 8 November they met to hear an invited speaker, Mr. Peter Barwick, who had organised and completed a self-build project at Crawley in 1966, explaining the problems of self-build.

Only the male members of the families involved were present.[8] At the meeting they decided to form a Steering Committee of six members, with Mike Lundberg as Chairman, and to take advice from the National Federation of Housing Associations. Lundberg had previously approached the local District Council and reported to the meeting that the Council seemed to be willing to support a self-build scheme with land and finance. The meeting decided that the scheme should be for twenty houses, with 3 or 4 bedrooms and garages, and that the materials cost should be about £5,000 each. The group also agreed to pay into a fund to build up a stock of materials and buy the necessary tools and plant.

Following this meeting Mr. Barwick wrote an impassioned letter to the local newspaper[9] pleading for more recognition by central and local government of the potential for self-build housing provision, and asking for help by making land and finance more easily available. He pointed out that most self-builders were either Council tenants or on their waiting lists, and therefore completed self-build schemes would make Council houses available for re-letting at no cost to the Councils involved. In the case of Downsview group this plea was to remain unheeded for nearly one year.

One important event for self-builders was the screening by BBC Television of a documentary on self-help in housing in 1974. The self-build case shown was an example of the Colin Wadsworth Group schemes in Yorkshire. Wadsworth had learned about self-building the hard way. In the documentary he described how he had formed a self-build group in 1963 and the many mistakes he and his group had made in choosing their site and setting up their organisation. His desire to use this experience to make sure that self-builders did not make the same mistakes led him to set up an organisation which would give groups a professional management service.[10] The most important point he stressed was that without land available there was really no point in forming a self-build group. Although some of the Downsview group had seen the BBC film, the Wadsworth message on land and organisation did not seem to have been fully appreciated.

During the next six months the group gave up their free time with their families to meet most weekends. With the help of one of their members, a draughtsman, they drew up house plans, and they shopped around for reasonably priced materials, mainly timber, and built up a stock of scaffolding. During this time they also made formal approaches to the Thamesdown Borough and North Wilts District Council for allocation of land and sent enquiries to estate agents throughout the area. But none of these approaches produced any result, neither Council seemed to want the trouble of dealing with a part-time building development with no corporate status. In the case of Thamesdown, this was surprising as they had previously helped self-build groups in the late 1950's and early 1960's. The prolonged search for suitable land had a demoralising effect on the members. The continual meetings to discuss their housing designs with no building plots to relate to began to cause friction among the members. Several times it seemed as if they would break up in desperation at the delays, and it was only the dogged determination and optimistic leadership of Lundberg which kept them together.

In May 1975, after reading local newspaper reports of the advisory work of the Centre for Alternatives in Urban Development, the Downsview Secretary wrote to the Centre asking for help. At about the same time the group had started negotiations with an estate agent for a suitable piece of land which was being sold by order of the Official Receiver. This land had already been partly develped with a road layout, drainage and some house foundations.

It seemed a perfect situation, and had the support of the local Council for planning permission and finance for the development process, including the cost of the land. The group put in an offer for the land but were told by the agent that they were now bidding against another potential purchaser. They increased their offer and notified the District Valuer of the amount. It required his approval before submission could be made to the Council for their support for public funds to be allocated under the terms of the Housing Act 1957. The group also negotiated with a Building Society for mortgage facilities to their members for the individual house purchase, once the houses had been completed. The time taken to complete these formalities was so drawn out that they lost the land to a competing bidder. To have got so near to land purchase and then failed had a very bad effect on the group's morale. Again, it was only the determination of their Chairman which kept them together. But by the time they met representatives of CAUD on 10 June 1975 their numbers were reduced to ten. They were assured that the Centre would do everything in its power to help them acquire suitable building land, and promised my services in providing technical and organisational help free, under the terms of the Anglo-German Foundation grant. The following week I met the Chairman and Secretary of the group and strongly advised them to affiliate to the National Federation of Housing Associations and register under the Industrial and Provident Societies Act 1965. This would incorporate them as a limited liability company and give them a constitution acceptable to the local authorities.[11] Downsview Self-Build Housing Association Ltd. was duly registered on 15 July 1975 and a letterhead was printed with the name and registration number and the Secretary's name and address. It was noticeable that from this time on they were treated more seriously by the authorities concerned.

The members of the group were invited to the Summer School in September and were able to meet informally with officers and elected members of the Thamesdown Borough, and to discuss their problems with them. They played an important part in the Summer School workshops and impressed everyone by their exposition of the problems of a self-build group in its early stages. There is little doubt that the goodwill they established during those two weeks helped them to gain the confidence of the Thamesdown officials. The officials, however, had implied that they would require the group to have some professional back-up before they would give it their full support.

So Downsview wrote to the Centre formally requesting this backing, and it was agreed that I should give them the professional consultancy required.

Later in September the Borough of Thamesdown wrote to Downsview offering 12 individual plots at South Dorcan and requested a meeting to discuss the matter.

This meeting turned out to be only the start to a long period of negotiations on the final price of the land and the granting of loan sanction. The group also had to go through a long series of interviews with Building Societies to arrange for mortgage facilities for the eventual purchase of the individual houses by their members.

During this time I had been discussing their original house design with them and it soon became apparent that it was too ambitious and too costly.

Their original budget estimate of £5,000 for materials per house was too low for the area of their preferred design of some 1800 square feet on two floors. It took a lot of persuasion on my part to get them to realise that they could neither afford to build nor maintain a house of that size. But it was not until they saw the plots in South Dorcan that they finally realised they would have to scale the houses down to an area of about 1200 square feet. I also advised them that the services of an architect would be needed to finalise the designs, negotiate for planning and building regulations permissions, and certify the work for stage payments by the local authority. In December an architect[12] was commissioned with a written agreement of the services they would require from him and sketch designs were soon produced and discussed. It was only the discussions about these designs and the feeling that at last they might get the houses built in the near future that kept up their morale during the ensuing months. By April 1976 the plans had been approved by the local authority and the price of the land finally settled. But it took another six months for the land to be conveyed, the mortgage documents drawn up, and the methods of stage finance to be arranged. It was this frustrating waiting time that proved to be the last straw for Mike Lundberg. The man who had held the group together for so long resigned and went his own way. Bill Carlton, the Secretary, was appointed Chairman in his place and his intelligent and good humoured leadership helped the group to complete their scheme in record time. In the early part of November the Downsview members took their tools and equipment on site and commenced building, two years, almost to the day, after their first meeting.

By this time the group consisted of 12 members, ten of whom were married with one or more children, and two who were engaged to be married. Four were carpenters, two bricklayers, two plumbers, one electrician, one plasterer, one excavator driver and one groundworker.

The Dorcan site was ideal as it could accommodate 12 houses of two storeys

8

with integral garages and still have enough space left for good sized gardens. After discussions with their architect, the group decided on two house types to meet their various needs and choices.

The type of construction and its design, usually called 'traditional', was chosen by Downsview because they had the necessary tradesmen in the group to carry it out. But it was also recognised that it would be both acceptable to the planning authority for the South Dorcan Area and also to the potential market on resale. This marketability aspect is important to many self-builders who see this way of building as a first step on the home-ownership 'ladder'.

The building of the houses was organised under a set of working regulations recommended by the NFHA Self-Build Manual. The Manual is a guide to all aspects of the organisation, such as committee structure, relationships with consultants, accounts and auditing, etc.[13] But self-build groups have to learn to some extent from their mistakes, and Downsview was no exception. In their case these were mainly financial rather than structural.

Downsview had the initial problem of working on the foundations and site works in the face of winter. They decided to buy a small excavator and were lucky enough to have an experienced driver as a member. They dug the foundations for four houses very quickly and decided to sub-contract the brickwork to try and get the shells up and roofs on before the worst of the winter weather. They were again lucky to have an experienced bricklayer in the group who decided to work full-time with paid help as the sub-contractor. As little or no work could be done by members in the evenings because of lack of daylight, this arrangement suited them at first, but its continuation into spring and summer was their first big mistake.

Sub-contract labour drains away funds which should be used for materials and plant and should only be used when the skills are not available in the group. Here members' skills were being used on a sub-contract basis and not on a group working basis, and were thus a misuse of internal manpower resources.

The group were advised to buy and check and store their materials carefully. This they did in the early stages, but once on site the pressure of work gradually disrupted this part of their organisation. This resulted in their buying materials at a higher rate than warranted in a depressed market, and the wastage on site was greater than it need have been. This was their second big mistake and added up to a considerable financial waste which they could ill afford.

9

On the whole, the group worked well together, and by May 1977 they had the roofs on 5 houses and could work on the interiors during wet weather. By this time they had the rest of the foundation work out of the ground and most of the drainage runs completed. It was a remarkable achievement to have made such good progress despite the wet winter and early spring weather.

During May, I carried out a review of the development with some of the members of the group. The following points emerged:

(a) It was acknowledged that they had not realised the importance of competitive material buying. At this late date they had now appointed the most 'commercial' minded member of the group to take on this task.

(b) Despite the advice given, they had not programmed the work in such a way that it was linked to the cost of each operation. They were now trying to arrange this so that the members could see that the smooth flow of progress would mean saving in time and an earlier completion date. At the high interest rates they were paying on money loaned, this would be an important factor in the final cost.

(c) House allocation had been made before building started and this meant that some members had tended to concentrate work on their own houses rather than on the scheme as a whole. It was agreed that house allocation should not have been made until the first house was ready for occupation.

(d) The decision to allow 'extras' — additional finishes and equipment — was regretted. This had held up progress on the basic design and cost the whole group money. It was now too late to stop this, but they agreed that 'extras' should have been the responsibility of individual households after completion of the whole scheme.

(e) They were dissatisfied with the performance of one member as General Foreman. They had lost production time from this member and had not gained any extra progress in return for his general supervision time. They were now considering the appointment of working trade 'leaders' who would be responsible for quality and progress in their own trades.

By this time they had realised the mistakes of their earlier sub-contract and had agreed to sub-contract only the roof tiling and glazing.

By the late summer of 1977 half the houses were occupied and paying rent to the group as agreed under their rules. In December two more houses were occupied, and by early February 1978 all the houses were complete and occupied, the total time for construction being 15 months. The site works, driveways, fences and general clearing up were completed by the early summer, an exceptionally wet winter having delayed these. Now this work is complete and the mortgages for purchase finalised the group can wind up, and this should take place sometime during the summer.

There is no doubt that the Downsview members have achieved their goal of owning a good sized, well-built and equipped and marketable house. Unlike most other self-build groups, and despite their mistakes, they achieved this with the minimum of trouble on site and in an unusually short time.

Most self-build groups usually take at least 2 years[14] and experience many difficulties on site. What is exceptional in the Downsview case, is the amount of time it took them to find land and, despite this, how they managed to stay together as a viable group.

In my view, the earlier use of some professional management and technical help could have helped overcome some of Downsview's initial difficulties, but the support of local authorities and other government agencies is also absolutely necessary. The Government recognised this in its Self-Build Circular, but the message is slow to reach these agencies. In the case of Thamesdown the officers were very co-operative, but there were still long and frustrating delays before the land was conveyed. It would seem that the kind of help and advice given in a limited way by the Centre must be available on a wider basis if self-build is to play a significant part in the provision of housing.

The original estimate of cost for each house, excluding land and the member's labour content, was approximately £9,000.[15] The final cost is likely to be £12,000, the excess of £2,500 made up of 'extras' as described earlier; sub-contract work not originally accounted for; and materials bought at inflated prices.

Informal valuations by the local authority and Building Society surveyors have put the market value of the houses at between £18,000 and £20,000. While these valuations cannot be tested unless a house is put onto the market, the usual estimate of savings by members' labour is in the order of one third of the market value. Downsview appears to have achieved this objective with something in hand. The members are now negotiating their individual mortgages, these vary considerably according to the amount they are able and prepared to put down, and are preparing to wind up the association.

When I visited them in late Spring, I found all the families busy finishing off the painting work and planting the gardens. The wives seemed highly satisfied with the standards of space and equipment, the good sized gardens and spacious site layout of the houses. The men were proud of their achievement and more than satisfied with the financial results.

4.   TOOTHILL SELF-BUILD HOUSING ASSOCIATION LTD.

An article in Ideal Home magazine in 1975 carried the following headline text "So You Think You Could Build Your Own House . . . well, it's one way of fighting inflation, high interest rates and soaring land costs; but approach with caution. It can often mean months of time and money wasted, wrangling with local authorities, it certainly means exhausting evenings, weekends and holidays on site, it sometimes ends in disappointment through no fault of the group or individuals. . . ." Not only did the text carry a timely warning of the efforts required by the Toothill Self-Builders, but its prophesy of disappointments to come was unfortunately true in their case.

At the CAUD/AA Summer School there had been much discussion on the use of simpler forms of construction for self-build groups. The Downsview group were typical of most self-builders throughout England, in that they preferred to use the more "traditional" means of construction, bricks and mortar, because it produced a predictable and marketable product. Walter Segal, in his Summer School lecture, had shown his audience that construction by simple timber frame methods could reduce the building time by as much as two thirds with the consequent savings in cost and self-builders' time on the site.

At my meetings with the Borough officers in the Autumn of 1975, I had been assured that land would be allocated and support given to a self-build group using new methods in the Toothill development area in the Western expansion of Thamesdown.

So undue 'wrangling' with the local authority was seen to be not a problem in the setting up of such a project. What I had to do was to try to convince the prospective self-builders that a simpler method of construction was to their advantage.

In the period January to July 1976 the Centre received a number of enquires from people interested in forming a self-build group, many of them referred to us by Downsview. During the same period the Borough of Thamesdown had been developing the Toothill area,[16] and most of the road layout design had been completed ready for plot allocation. On 26 July the Borough wrote to the Centre offering a self-build site and suggesting that building should commence early in 1977. Because of this positive offer we now felt that we could call together all those people who had expressed interest, and a meeting was arranged for mid-August. Twelve replies were received to a circular letter accepting the invitation to the meeting, and on the appointed evening seven men turned up, three of them with their wives. Bill Carlton, the Chairman of Downsview, had been invited to address the meeting, and he gave details of Downsview's history, problems and proposed scheme. He also mentioned how interested he had been in Segal's ideas at the Summer School, but was not able to interest his own group in them as they had already made the basic decisions on design and construction.

The outcome af the meeting was a decision to find more participants, publicise the ideas of self-build through the local press, and meet again the following month. The local newspaper ran a report of the meeting and this brought a further response from interested people.

The second meeting was held at the Centre in September, and Peter Barwick, the man who had helped Downsview previously, showed slides and explained his 1966 Crawley Self-Build project. This project had been constructed in the bricks and mortar 'traditional' style and had taken over two years to complete. The early slides showed a site covered in mud with building materials scattered all over the place, a set of images almost certain to discourage most potential self-builders. In the discussion following the lecture the audience of six men with their wives and children asked if there could be easier ways of building a house. I promised to obtain slides of a house designed by Segal and built by a man and his wife, with no building skills, in four months at a cost of £4,000 in 1971.[17] These slides, and a tape recording of Segal's Summer School lecture, were presented to the same audience in October and the group seemed convinced that this was the sort of construction they wanted. It was decided to hold a business meeting later that month to discuss formal registration and membership fees. This meeting was, in fact, very businesslike. A Chairman, Secretary and Treasurer were elected, and six families agreed to pay an initial membership fee of £5. I was asked to write to the Borough's Capital Projects Manager to request that he meet the group in December to explain the land position and confirm Borough's promised support.

They also asked me to notify the National Federation of Housing Associations of their intentions and obtain the necessary registration forms and model rules.

It was also decided to investigate, on site, the two main construction methods which had been presented to the group and so arrangements were made for visits to the Downsview site at Dorcan, and a house Walter Segal was building in North London.

One Saturday in November a number of the members went to visit the Segal house site in North London. This house was the first two-story timber framed house Segal had designed and built, and he wanted the group to see it as their preference at that time was for two floors. The members were very impressed by the ease of construction, the finish of the materials and especially by the minimum amount of ground works. Excavation was confined to 2 feet square holes for the timber posts and two main drain runs. The rest of the site, an existing garden, had been left untouched and the whole operation was neat and tidy.

A different picture was presented at the Downsview site, it was similar to the scenes they had seen in the Crawley slides, a mess of excavation, earth moving and mud! It was only the skill of the excavator driver which kept the site in any kind of order.

By the time of the next meeting a majority of the group had decided on a timber-framed two-story house using the Segal methods, the site visits had convinced them of the most suitable method of construction.

In December the Capital Projects Manager met the group at the Centre and gave them a full picture of the plans for the Toothill area; the proposed schools, shops, social centre, churches, pubs and types of housing. He explained how the Borough would allocate and convey the land, and asked for an early meeting with the members and their consultants to discuss the short term borrowing arrangements for the construction. It was also explained to them how to apply for the mortgages they would require at the end of the building process. The group declared their interest in the Segal type of construction, and the Capital Projects Manager agreed to support this kind of design proposal. The meeting closed in a very optimistic mood.

At their next meeting in January 1977 the group decided to register as a self-build society and affiliate to the National Federation of Housing Associations. Each couple agreed to pay £21 towards registration and administration costs, and £5 per week thereafter to buy tools and equipment. By this time the group numbered five families with one or more children, and four couples engaged to be married. The families lived in Council property and the engaged couples were to be first-time home buyers. None of the members had any building skills.

They agreed to meet on a fortnightly basis at the house of the Chairman, and asked me to give them advice as and when necessary.

In mid-January the group had received site plans from the Borough, and they asked me to explain the situation to Walter Segal with a view to his appointment as their architect. Segal agreed to be present at the meeting arranged with the Thamesdown officers, and discuss his designs and methods with them.

On 3 February 1977 the Chairman and Secretary, Segal and I met the Capi-

14

tal Projects Manager and his staff at the Borough offices. Segal showed slides of his houses, both single and two-storey, and the reaction of the Thamesdown officers was enthusiastic. They were keen to see new ideas being tried out in the Toothill area, and did not anticipate any planning or building regulations problems. Walter Segal's personality impressed itself upon them and his long experience as an architect led them to trust him with new ideas. It was agreed that the Toothill Self-Build Group should enter into formal agreements on land price and building finance as soon as possible, using the formula already worked out with Downsview. The meeting ended with expressions of goodwill all round.

After the meeting Segal agreed to work out various sketch designs, based on the requirements, and to submit these for consideration as soon as possible. In the meantime the group would negotiate the price of the land with the Borough.

By 16 February agreement in principle was reached; the site was to be approximately 1 acre, laid out in 11 single house plots, and the price of £30,000 was to include roads, kerbs and main drainage.

By the third week in February the group had received and considered the architect's various sketch proposals, and it was decided to meet him to finalise the scheme. On 26 February the group travelled to London to meet Segal at his office and after a long discussion made these decisions:

— That the houses should all be based on the same plan of 1,000 square feet, as the window and door openings could then be varied as necessary within the same timber frame. A single storey was preferred now by everyone in the group.
— That the basic cost was to be no more than £7,000 per house, excluding the cost of land and professional fees.
— That the group would use the architect's services to provide advice on materials buying, storage arrangements, work programming and the purchase of appropriate tools. This continuing advice was considered to be necessary as there were no building skills within the group.
— That no women and children were to be allowed on site as this would increase the insurance premiums.

On 11 March the group was registered as Toothill Self-Build Housing Association Ltd. and able to enter into formal contracts. On 15 May Walter Segal received a letter of appointment and instructions to finalise his design ready for submission for planning permission. He was also authorised to appoint a Quantity Surveyor to cost the design for loan finance approval from

15

the local authority.

By this time the composition of the group had changed somewhat; it was now comprised of 4 families and 7 engaged couples, the other families having left for various reasons. These were because they had found suitable houses immediately available elsewhere, at the right price; because they were not sure that they could afford the mortgage payments; or because their need for another house was not urgent enough to warrant the amount of physical work the scheme would demand. However, the decision by the core group to allow the proponderance of engaged couples who replaced them proved to be a fatal one, unforeseen by anyone at the time.

The Architect and the Quantity Surveyor worked quickly, the only change in design being to a flat roof for reasons of cost. On 27 May the group and myself met the Thamesdown officers with all the necessary information to finalise the negotiations. Present at the meeting were the Borough's legal, estates, and finance officers and agreement was reached on all matters of finance and conveyancing of the land and the final drawings and site layouts were approved for submission to the planning committee. The format of the Schedule of Costs was agreed, on the Downsview model, and the group agreed to have this completed for a housing committee resolution for loan sanction on 2 June. When completed the Schedule totalled just over £9,500 per house, including land and other charges. It was a little higher than the group had budgeted for but this time there was no feeling that it was too much for any member of the group to pay.

It was a remarkable achievement to have brought a self-build group together, designed a suitable house for them, completed land and planning negotiations with the local authority, and agreed on cost and loan sanction, all within the space of about six months. The house had been designed to be constructed in less than six months, and was estimated to have a final market value of around £15,000.

Two combined factors were, however, to bring this achievement to nothing. Firstly, the majority of members in the group were engaged couples (7:5); and secondly, the speculative house builders in Thamesdown were not selling their houses quickly enough.

During June 1977 a speculative building company placed a series of advertisements in the Swindon Evening Advertiser aimed at first time house buyers and engaged couples. Two bedroom houses were offered at prices between £8,550 and £9,595 with mortgages arranged. Various financial inducements were offered to close the gap between the mortgage obtained and the total cost of the houses, and on paper the propositions seemed attractive. They were certainly attractive enough to unsettle the engaged couples in the group who were eager to start married life. They could see the houses they were being offered, and they knew exactly what their financial commitments would be and they could move in almost immediately.

At the meeting on 19 June all seven engaged couples voted to leave the group. They stated that the houses now available on the market were suitable for their needs, at least for the time being, and they wanted to be free to buy them. There was little the family members could do to stop the group breaking up, other than insisting on the engaged couples paying their dues towards the costs already incurred. So, reluctantly, on 20 June the Chairman notified the Capital Projects Manager of the position and relinquished the claim to the land. No contracts had been signed and there was no legal obligation on either side. The Thamesdown officers were very disappointed, they had seen the scheme "breaking new ground" for them, but they were unable to hold the land until the group had time to re-form.

So two lessons learned from this experience were:

(a) That a family self-build group should allow only a minimum of engaged couples (in the case of Downsview it was two), as any delay tends to unsettle their loyalty to the group.

(b) That a self-build group should have, and continue to use, available advice on its composition and organisation as well as on construction matters. From the time of its registration the group did not take my advice and only used me as a link with the architect and the local authority. Perhaps if they had been paying a fee, under a service contract, they would have demanded and used my advice more effectively.

The Toothill Self-Build Association is still in being, with a core group of some of the original families. They do not intend to let the group numbers increase to over seven members until they have purchased land and designed a house suitable for the site. They will then advertise for more members who will have to accept the design and site already agreed. They also intend to demand a higher weekly subscription from their members of about £10 per week and thus make it much more difficult for members to consider leaving the group than previously. They are convinced that land prices in the area will come down in price from their present inflated value and are watching the market keenly. My impression is that they will build these houses eventually and that they will be much more careful at each stage of their development, particularly with regard to their membership after the painful lessons they learned.

5. TOOTHILL CO-OPERATIVE DWELLINGS LTD.

A further outcome of the Summer School was the decision by the Centre to ask the Borough of Thamesdown for an updating of their 1974 report on residential accommodation requirements for single people.[18] The result was a clear indication of the need for more single-person provision within the Borough, for all categories, and especially in the newly developing Western area.

In the light of this survey, the Centre decided to contact interested single people in Thamesdown, as well as institutions and companies who employed numbers of single people, to meet and discuss the proposal to build a housing co-operative scheme to meet their needs.

The response was encouraging, and the institutions and companies were enthusiastic about the possiblities of more accommodation for their single students and employees. In December 1975 a meeting was convened in Swindon for single people, or their representatives, to hear the proposals and give their views. Although a great deal of interest had been generated only ten people turned up at the meeting. However, these ten were representative of single people in education, commerce and industry, and their ages ranged from 20 years to 55 years. The main purpose of the meeting was to discuss in some depth the opinions expressed on the personal requirements for single person accommodation and to tape record these opinions as the start of the design brief. The discussion was based on the Department of the Environment Design Bulletins for single people under retirement age, the only guidelines available at that time.[19]

The discussion which followed was lively and well informed, all the participants gave their views in some detail and the results of the 3½ hour meeting were conclusive enough to provide a brief for sketch designs. Before the meeting broke up five of the participants had agreed to form a Steering Committee as the nucleus of the Co-operative.

In January 1976 the Government published its Circular on Housing Co-operatives and this formed the basis for further discussions with Thamesdown. By the end of January the Centre was able to present proposals to the Borough's Project Management Division on behalf of the Co-operative and alternative sites in the Toothill area were discussed as to their suitability. Later that month, John Turner and I met John Hands at the Society for Co-operative Dwellings in London to seek his advice on the formation of the Co-operative and its possible affiliation to a servicing agency.[20]

Following this meeting it was decided to recommend to the Steering Committee that they should affiliate to SCD and form the Development Committee of a primary non-equity co-operative as recommended in the Circular.[21]

In March the Steering Committee held its first meeting at the Centre and elected a Chairman and invited me to act as non-voting Secretary. I reported on the meetings with the Thamesdown officers and described the proposed allocation of land at Toothill. I also reported on the meetings with John Hands and recommended affiliation with the Society for Co-operative Dwellings. The Committee resolved to affiliate to SCD and name itself Toothill Co-operative Dwellings Development Committee, it was also agreed that the architect who had been advising the Centre[22] be asked to prepare an outline scheme for submission to Thamesdown in consultation with the Committee.

At the beginning of April the Minister for Housing and Construction, Mr. Reg Freeson, visited Thamesdown and formally opened the first Council houses for occupation in the Toothill area. In his public speech he declared support for a housing co-operative development in Toothill. This support was echoed by the Borough's Chairman of Policy and Resources Committee and the Chairman of the Housing Committee, and it was felt that the Toothill Co-operative could begin to make real progress. Unfortunately this optimism was not borne out by the 2 years of prolonged negotiations which followed.

At the end of April the SCD affiliation was formally agreed and a meeting was arranged between the Borough's Capital Project Manager, the Toothill Development Committee, and SCD's Development Officer.

At the meeting concern was expressed over the lack of any formal intent in writing by the Borough for a co-operative scheme, but we were assured by the Capital Projects Manager that this would be forthcoming. The 4 acre site was discussed, along with housing densities, car parking, and the Borough's nomination rights to a number of tenancies in the Co-operative. SCD's Development Officer reiterrated concern about the lack of formal written intent, and the meeting was generally inconclusive, but it was agreed that the architect should submit the Development Committee's requirements in the form of a sketch layout as soon as possible. SCD would then decide if it could support the scheme before negotiating with the Borough on behalf of the Development Committee. This sketch layout was sent to SCD later in May, and the Architect emphasised that it expressed the 'user' requirements as instructed by the Development Committee and did not necessarily accept all the constraints implied by government planning and costing regulations a this stage. During June no progress was recorded, there was no letter of intent from the Borough and no response from SCD, so in July the Chairman called a meeting of the Development Committee to consider how they could make progress. Despite the lack of support from SCD they agreed to proceed with the detailed design of the scheme and find ways to involve more single people in the design discussions. Renewed contact would be made with all those people who had shown interest in the first meeting with a view to incorporating their views into the final scheme. Another public meeting was then held in August at which the Architect explained the scheme and decisions on the final details were discussed and agreed by all present. The Development Committee was enlarged to eleven members, and made more representative of single people in the area. The meeting also asked me to contact the Director of Development and Housing (Borough of Thamesdown) to obtain a clear letter of intent on the financing of the scheme. During the later part of August and during September I had three informal meetings with the Director and his Capital Projects Manager to discuss this financial commitment; they in turn had informal discussions with the Department of the Environment South West Region to try to get financial support in written form for the scheme from central Government.

During this time the Architect was working on the detailed design and presented it to the Development Committee in October who agreed to submit the drawings to the Borough for planning permission together with a letter asking for an early decision on financial support.

Later in October the Capital Projects Manager wrote to inform the Department of the Environment South West Region of the intention to build 70 single person units at Toothill at an estimated cost of approximately £500,000. He said that the Borough was unable to take the matter any further until they could obtain from the Department a broad approval in principle to public money being made available for such a scheme. He reminded the Department of the Minister's reference to the Co-operative in April, and said that the roads and sewers to the site would be completed in December. He concluded by pointing out that the Development Committee was having its next meeting at the end of the month and asking if some indication could be given urgently as to what course of action the DoE were able to take.

The Development Committee cancelled their October meeting as no further information was forthcoming, and this state of affairs continued throughout November. At the beginning of December I contacted an officer of the DoE in London to ask for help to break this deadlock, and was assured that finance had been allocated to the Co-operative but that further clarification of the scheme would have to come from the Borough to DoE South West Region. On 16 December the Development Committee met the Capital

Projects Manager who reported on his discussions with the Regional office. It was agreed that I should collaborate with him to draft a further submission of the scheme to the DoE.

Concern was expressed over the apparent lack of support from SCD on the sponsorship of the scheme and a decision was made to consider other sponsorship. It was resolved that an officer of the Borough be invited to join the Development Committee and the Capital Projects Manager agreed to discuss this with his Director.

In January 1977 I met the Capital Projects Manager to discuss the submission to the Department of the Environment. At the meeting it became apparent that the scheme could not be developed further without the help of SCD as it would have to be sponsored by a registered housing association, but SCD still refused to be involved without a letter of intent. In February the Development Committee and the Borough decided to enlist the help of the Co-operative Housing Agency,[23] and received a letter from its Director to say that the DoE had agreed "in principle" that finance should be available for the scheme. This was followed in March by a letter from DoE South West Region saying that while no commitment to pay grant could be given at this early stage, provided the project satisfied the normal conditions, a project at Toothill would be eligible and that when the Co-operative had worked up a detailed scheme the DoE could then consider further the question of grant. Despite this letter SCD was still not altogether satisfied with the situation, or the viability of the scheme. By May the architect, deciding to continue work without a formal appointment, met the DoE Regional Architect to discuss the design and costs. He also submitted the scheme to Thamesdown for outline planning approval, and agreed to report back to the Development Committee on progress as soon as possible. During July to September the architect had a series of useful meetings with DoE South West Region. During this time the Development Committee Officers discussed the possibility of the Co-operative registering itself and proceeding with the scheme without sponsorship and met the Director of Development and Housing at Thamesdown to gain his support. The meeting was positive and the Director also promised Borough Officers representation on the Committee.

In November the Development Committee held its last meeting; there were three resignations and seven new members appointed. It heard reports of progress from the Chairman, Secretary and the Architect, and resolved unanimously to register as non-equity co-operative with the Register of Friendly Societies under the Industrial and Provident Societies Act 1965, and to affiliate to the National Federation of Housing Associations. Seven members agreed to become Founder members of Toothill Co-operative Dwellings Ltd.,

21

and the other seven members agreed to serve on the Management Committee of the new association.

In December 1977 the first meeting of the Management Committee of Toothill Co-operative Dwellings Ltd. took place in Swindon. The former Chairman of the Development Committee was elected as Secretary and election of the other officers was deferred until after registration was completed. The architect was formally appointed, conditional upon scheme approval, and it was agreed to ask SCD and AHAS (Associated Housing Advisory Services) for a specification of their services as potential servicing agents. I resigned from the Committee because of a conflict of interest as I was now a founder-partner of AHAS.[24] On 2 February the Co-operative was formally registered with the Registrar of Friendly Societies.

The Management Committee met again in February to elect a Chairman and Treasurer and co-opt the Capital Projects Manager to represent the Borough. They also invited AHAS to attend the meeting to present their management services and costs in more detail.

AHAS were then unanimously appointed as servicing agents, conditional upon scheme approval, and the Capital Projects Manager assured the Committee that the scheme was now certain to go ahead. AHAS was instructed to apply to the Housing Corporation for registration of the Co-operative as a Housing Association; to the DoE for scheme approval; and to the Borough for the acquisition of the land. The architect was instructed to submit planning application for the final agreed scheme and for the development of the site. It was also agreed that, with the help of AHAS, the Co-operative should begin to recruit potential tenant members.

This prolonged and frustrating pre-development period of the Toothill Co-operative seems to be typical in the relatively new housing co-operative movement. It was recognised by the Government in its Circular that adequate advice and support were crucial to co-operative developments, especially in their initial stages. The lack of knowledge of the best procedures by all concerned, and the suspicion of co-operatives by many people have certainly been a constraint on reasonable progress. Despite the enthusiasm and support from the Borough of Thamesdown it was difficult to make progress through the bureaucratic channels. It was hoped that the establishment of the Co-operative Housing Agency would do much to alleviate this situation but the Agency's lack of funds and adequate power has not enabled them to help very much, except in the educational field. Lack of funds to pay for professional advice during their pre-development has meant that many Co-Ops cannot proceed without sponsoring associations.

These associations are not always sympathetic to local users' needs, and will not do speculative work unless they are assured of the scheme's eventual backing. Toothill Co-operative was lucky enough to have some of the professional advice it needed paid for by the Anglo-German Foundation, and fortunate to have a sympathetic Architect who was prepared to suffer all the difficulties without a formal appointment.

At the time of writing it is still not certain that Toothill Co-operative Dwellings Scheme will be built and occupied by its members, and the Government cannot expect the enthusiasm and involvement it is asking from the housing co-operative movement unless it lifts some of the frustrating and time consuming bureaucratic constraints.

6.   QUESTIONS, SUGGESTIONS, AND AN EXPERIMENT

In the three Swindon case studies only the Downsview project has come to a successful conclusion so far, the Toothill Self-Build Group are still searching for ways and means to put their ideas into practice; and the Toothill Co-operative story is still a long way from its final chapter.

In the latter part of 1978 I shall be carrying out an evaluation of the Downsview scheme and hope to show how much of a success story it is, and what lessons it has for similar groups in social and financial terms. The Toothill Self-Builders are optimistic about their future but are proceeding with caution and a better understanding of the problems they will have to face; how to find land at the right price, and how to organise the group more effectively. The Toothill co-operative is still beset by many problems, most of them of a bureaucratic nature, and at present it is impossible to foresee what the outcome of that project will be. This is typical of many groups I have come across recently who are looking to co-operatives as a way of solving their housing needs, only to find that the legal and financial barriers take so much time and effort to overcome that they find it difficult to keep together and retain their initial enthusiasm.

Despite some reservations, I am convinced that the assumptions on which we set up the Centre for Alternatives in Urban Development were correct; that there is a pent-up demand for co-operative and self-help action in housing and local development that can be released when government, people, and independent agents work together; and that direct and indirect costs can be significantly lowered as a result.

I am sure that the major constraints are institutional and bureaucratic, and not technological. There are readily available techniques highly appropriate for use by individuals, small groups, and local enterprises for new and improved construction, and for its management on completion.

I am also convinced there are many people able and willing to invest considerable time and effort in using these when given the opportunity, in spite of the often great administrative barriers in their way. I believe, in the changing climate of opinion increasingly co-incident in the main political parties, that the necessary structural changes in law and administrative procedures are becoming possible; and that the opportunities and resources for people to work on their own housing would therefore increase thus leaving the 'supplied' sector for people who are unable, or unwilling, to do this.

From these tentative conclusions, and the case studies which led me to them, certain questions are raised relating to the wider issues.

24

The self-help and co-operative practices described in this report raise the issues of work and employment in the building industry and the social services and these, in turn, highlight the even broader question of the government of housing and the role of professionals. Those employed in the construction industry and in government and government supported housing agencies are bound to feel that their livelihoods could be threatened by a large increase of self-help and co-operative methods. If these methods, which have such an evident potential, especially for lower income households, were to increase substantially, the direction of change and development in the housing system as a whole would change. Self-build would increase the effective demand for construction materials, equipment and furnishings; contracts for co-operative housing would increase effective demands for small and medium-sized builders. These changes would bring about a redistribution of work and employment but would they lead to a net decrease of a net increase? What sectors would be affected and how?

The greatly increased share of responsibility that self-help builders and co-operating groups take for their housing has profound implications for the relationships of people, government and mediating professionals. Intermediaries cannot be agents of central organisations supplying goods and services, instead they must become mediators in the processes by which local people obtain the resources they need for providing their own housing. The cases reported represent a major change in the nature of this demand and of government response; from demands for centrally supplied housing to demands for access to resources for locally supplied housing which households themselves determine.

Are these demands and attitudes expressed peculiar to small minorities or particular kinds of people? Or do these groups represent a widespread potential for change? If so, as I and my colleagues believe, then how can we, and others like us, make the transition from dependent agents of corporate suppliers to independent mediators at the service of ordinary people enabled by government, to act for themselves.

At the present time we have no accurate information on what the effective demand from self-help is, or could be, and this information is necessary before we can attempt to answer the question of what scale of change in the redistribution of work and employment these practices would bring about.

We know that self-help provides a market for building materials and equipment, and that building materials manufacturers and suppliers recognise this.[25] The substantial increase in supply outlets for Do-It-Yourself materials in the last few years is proof of this. Manufacturers have also developed more materials and tools which are easy for unskilled people to use, and are seeking markets for these. The local networks for the distribution of the materials and equipment are well established and efficiently organised, and they keep a large number of people in employment. What we do not know is how a substantial increase in self-help housing would affect their markets overall.

The skilled building worker, the small and medium-sized building firm, and the professionals involved in housing would also be affected, but to what extent is not clear at the present time.

We do know that most self-build groups will need skilled help and professional advice, and that housing co-operatives will have to contract out most of their work, and certainly will require professional help in design, management and legal matters. Again, what we do not know is how much a substantial increase in self-help activity will affect the livelihoods of the people in this sector.

I suggest that what is needed now is: an overall survey of the effective demand with a special bias on priorities and pent-up demand; and a careful monitoring of existing schemes in their development stages, followed by an evaluation of completed projects. These should produce at least the basic information we need to begin to answer some of the questions raised above.

I have already said that I am convinced that there is a pent-up demand for co-operative and self-help action in housing and local development that can be realised when government, people and independent agents work together. What I am not sure of is how large this demand is or how much it represents a widespread potential for change.

I think it is necessary, therefore, to carry out the investigations I have already suggested, but also I think some experimental work is needed to test what changes are possible in the working relationships with government when people take a greatly increased responsibility for their housing.

My suggestion is that this work should be in the form of action-research, or "learning by doing", carried out by independent agents working with identified self-help groups. The research would test the following hypotheses:

— Firstly, that housing can only act as a vehicle for economic and social betterment when it is a locally controlled activity, as distinct from a centrally administered commodity;

— Secondly, that housing technologies and management must therefore be appropriate for use by small enterprises, and;

— Thirdly, that government roles should be limited to supporting local action, principally by guaranteeing equitable access to basic resources (especially land and finance) and the provision of infrastructure and services.

The method used by mediating agents would be that of participant/observer, making it possible for them to take part in activities already going on, while at the same time making available certain needed skills and assisting in the transfer of these skills to the groups themselves. A monitoring and evaluation function would also be necessary to test the hypotheses and to make the experience available for the formation of other groups, creating a "learning-by-experience" situation.

On the question of how the transition can be made from agencies which are directly dependent upon centrally administered resources, to independent mediators at the service of ordinary people who are enabled by government to act for themselves, I would like to describe an experiment which was started by three colleagues and myself in 1977.

An experiment in mediation

I have found that governments tend to distrust local groups, especially if they are not led by certified professionals, and, on the other hand local groups, unaccustomed to dealing with government on equal terms, distrust its officials. To overcome these often unfounded fears I am sure more independent professionals with the appropriate attitudes and skills, are essential. As the work on the Swindon projects progressed I was certain that there would be a continuing need for the type of housing services I was providing in the self-build and co-operative housing fields. Not wanting to see my work, under the sponsorship of the Anglo-German Foundation, come to an abrupt end when the funding finished in January 1978, I proposed to my colleagues at the Centre that we should set up a fee-earning Housing Advisory service to continue the work.

I was influenced by a similar proposal by Richard Spohn in "Freedom to Build" for the setting up of such a service in California. This was to be funded initially by government to provide free advice, information and technical assistance to potential owner-builders of low and moderate incomes, and was seen to be the basis of a network of resources controlled by them.[26]

27

So I began working with John Turner[27] on the outline of a similar service for use within the context of British housing legislation. We were helped, to a great extent, by suggestions made by Peter McGregor, the Secretary General of the Anglo-German Foundation, who saw the possibility of such an organisation being instrumental in bringing changes to existing housing provision; and by Stan Windass who gave us much invaluable advice as well as financial help from the newly formed Foundation for Alternatives of which he was founder and director.

In those early days I saw the main emphasis of the service being placed on the needs of self-build groups. The work I was doing at that time with Walter Segal and the Toothill self-builders was seen as an important, innovative, development, the experience from which should be made available to intending self-builders elsewhere. But the temporary failure of the Toothill project, and the addition of two other members to the Team, Bertha Turner and Michael Drake,[28] changed this emphasis somewhat in the coming months as we began to look at the possibility of a wider scope for the service.

We were aware that there was a need to supplement the kinds of organisations that already existed but be flexible to work in partnership with them. We wanted to explore the opportunities for self-help with pilot schemes which demonstrated at the local level more economically and socially sound alternatives; and we wanted to find ways and means of transforming technical and management skills to local user groups to ensure their control over the resources available.

As a start we decided to form a company limited by guarantee with no shareholding, to be known as AHAS — Associated Housing Advisory Services. Its constitution gives the members continual equality on a co-operative basis and it is 'non-profit' in that any surpluses made are used only to improve the service and cannot be distributed.

It is through this organisation that we hope to carry out many of the tasks I have suggested. Some of them we are doing already: servicing two housing co-operatives in their pre-development stage; evaluating the Downsview self-build project; designing a self-build housing advice service; writing a contribution on housing to the IFDA (International Foundation for Development Alternatives) project for a U.N. development strategy for the 1980's and beyond; and designing a tenant mobility scheme for the public housing sector to be run on a co-operative basis.

This is all experimental work, as we are trying out ways and means which have not yet been fully tested. For instance, if we are allowed to continue to act as agents for the Toothill co-operative this will allow us to test ways of transferring skills to the members as quickly as possible; we shall also be able to monitor their progress and perhaps test the hypotheses I mentioned previously.

There has been no evaluation study made of a self-build group in this country, so the Downsview study should provide some vital information. If we get some initial finding for the self-build advice service this will enable us to investigate the resources available to these groups, help groups to form; and use the experience to structure a fee-earning service on a wider scale.

The contribution to the IFDA project will investigate selected case studies, from various countries, to consider an alternative strategy based on government *support* for locally self-reliant action as distinct from conventional policies in which housing goods and services are centrally *supplied*. The tenant mobility scheme is designed as a pilot project to enable tenants to overcome the acute difficulty they have at present of making a house transfer or exchange in the public housing sector. This transfer and exchange system will be controlled by the tenants in a series of co-operatives set up on the estates within a local authority housing area and working closely with the authority. Tenants and officials in two London Boroughs have agreed to collaborate in the initial project for which funding is being sought. If the experiment is successful then the co-operatives will eventually become self-financing.

In all this work we are trying out ways and means of setting up our mediating role. The present, and difficult, task is to find out how we can be employed by local users, rather than be the channel of resources over which they have little or no control and which makes them dependent upon those who should be serving them.

7. THE ORGANISATION OF SELF BUILD SOCIETIES

7.1 In the words of the Housing Act 1974, a Self-Build Society is defined as ". . . a housing association whose object is to provide for sale to, or occupation by, its members, dwellings built or improved principally with the use of its members' own labour. . ." [29] This was the first legislative recognition of this method of providing houses.

Our concern here is with the building of new houses and the only published guide mainly for the formation and management of groups for this purpose is the Manual for Self Build Housing Associations. [30] In the introduction to the manual, it is pointed out that the recognition of three basic requirements is essential for the success of any self-build group:

(i) That the rules and regulations should be designed in such a manner that the members are required to spend a very considerable part of their leisure each week on building activities.

(ii) That whilst their members are on site they have to be effectively organised and have an understanding of the jobs required to be done, as well as being enthusiastic and hard working.

(iii) That they should take care that their management policies do not dissipate the advantages of the first two requirements, either through ignorance or inexperience, and that their financial policy is controlled in such a manner as to gain the utmost benefit from the system.

The tone of the manual is rather authoritarian, but even so it is important to understand at the outset that these requirements are essential, whatever method of construction is used.

7.2 To obtain limited liability and gain access to available building finance, from whatever source, it is essential for a self build group to register with the Registrar of Friendly Societies under the Industrial and Provident Societies Act 1965. The Model Rules [31] provide for the legal objects and constitution of the Association, as well as its financial accounting obligations.

7.3 There is a legal minimum requirement of seven members, but from experience the most satisfactory number is between 10 and 20 members. The business of the Association is executed by a Committee of

Management consisting of a least seven members elected and answerable to the full membership in general meeting.

7.4 As the Association will be operating as a non-profit building company it is important that the necessary advice is taken;[32] a proper system of management is set up;[33] and an appropriate rule system is agreed so that members clearly understand their working obligations.

7.5 The appointment of a Solicitor is necessary for the processing of legal documents, such as the conveyancing of land and the compilation and execution of the Members' Working Agreement and the services of an Accountant may be required if there are no accounting skills available within the membership. Advice will almost certainly be necessary on tax considerations[34] and VAT.

7.6 Even if a Management Consultant is appointed it is essential that there is a full understanding by the members of their ultimate responsibility for making key decisions. It is in their own interests to make sure that land and materials are bought at the best price; that site working is conducted in the most suitable and efficient manner; and that sub-contractors are used only when absolutely necessary and at the most competitive prices.

7.7 The Working Regulations,[35] to which all members sign an Agreement, should cover the following items:

(i) The amount of Loan Stock and subscription required, payable in weekly or monthly instalments, to provide working capital and running expenses. This can amount to between £150 and £500 and is repayable on completion. In addition a £1 Ordinary Share is purchased for membership of the company.

(ii) The provision of insurance against death or injury; claims by third parties; theft, fire and other damage.

(iii) The job specification of each member, and the number of hours to be worked.

(iv) A method of recording the time worked and a procedure to deal with difficulties.

(v) A procedure to be adopted in the event of sickness.

(vi) The order of allocation of completed houses.

(vii) A form of Licence Agreement to occupy a completed house until such times as the whole scheme is finished and the houses sold to the individual members.

(viii) The amount of rent to be paid to the Association under the Licence.

(ix) The procedure for expulsion of a member.

These regulations can only be amended or rescinded once they have been passed by a two thirds majority of votes at a Special General Meeting of the Association as allowed for in the Model Rules.

7.8 Separate arrangements should be made with individual members who are elected to carry out specific duties such as: site foreman; materials ordering officer; safety and security officer; and trade team leaders.

These tasks are an essential part of the organisation and should be allocated carefully and fairly so that they are most conducive to the efficiency of the whole operation.

7.9 On completion of the scheme, and occupancy of all the houses by the members, the Association will be wound up under the terms set out in the Model Rules and the houses sold to the members. As this stage is approached, it is important that the Treasurer, together with the Association's auditor and solicitor, make an exact costing of each house and estimate the amounts of outstanding loans and charges. To this should be added a generous reserve to cover any bills or charges which may have accrued at the time of winding up. Once all the amounts are settled; individual building society mortgages granted to redeem the lending agency's loan; members loan stock repaid; and any surplus distributed to members; the Association can apply for dissolution.

8.   FINANCE AVAILABLE TO SELF-BUILD SOCIETIES

8.1 For the initial loan required to cover the cost of land, building materials and any sub-contract work, the most usual sources are the local authority, the Housing Corporation, a building society or a bank. When the scheme is completed each member arranges the finance for the purchase of his house, usually a mortgage through a building society.

8.2 Self Build Societies are eligible for loans from public funds and the Housing Act 1957[36] allows local authorities to lend money to them to cover the land and building costs. Before applying for loan sanction from the Department of the Environment to do this, the local authority will want to satisfy itself that the members are capable of carrying out the work to a satisfactory conclusion.

8.3 It is usual for the local authority officers to carry out a detailed examination of the financial status and character of the potential self-builders; of the skills they have within the membership; of the viability of their proposed housing development; and the knowledge and experience of their professional consultants.

8.4 Some local authorities will require that the members are existing council tenants, or on the housing list, or in housing need as a condition of financing the scheme.

8.5 The local authority will generally make the loan money available in six stages, which is a satisfactory arrangement for most types of construction. They will usually release the full amount for the purchase of the land and then capitalise the interest charges so that these become part of the final amount of the loan. Where they are providing the land, however, they may be prepared to allow the payment to be in stages but giving the right to occupy the whole site on commencement. This could reduce the interest costs considerably.

8.6 The Housing Corporation now has the statutory duty to promote and assist self-build societies, and is empowered to make loans to them.[37] The corporation is also empowered to acquire land for the purpose of selling or leasing it to a self-build society,[38] and where they are clearing land belonging to them and providing services they may occasionally be able to make part of the site available to a self-build group.[39]

8.7 It is not necessary for a self-build society providing dwellings for sale to its members to register with the Housing Corporation. However, this would be necessary if the scheme was for renting to members and

33

became eligible for housing association grant. [40]

8.8   Before agreeing to a loan the Housing Corporation will carry out a detailed examination of the group's status, in much the same way as a local authority. But they will tend to give preference to self-builders who are suffering stress with their present accommodation and will not lend to a group who appear to be interested only in creating a saleable asset.

8.9   The Housing Corporation will usually make the loan monies available for land and construction on a monthly basis. The payments must come within previously agreed cost limits and must be requested on properly invoiced and certified accounts. This means that the group's accounts and cost control systems must be accurate and up to date at all times. No loan request will be approved for the purchase of land if the asking price exceeds the value estimated by the District Valuer.

8.10 Building Societies do not usually make loans available for land purchase and so they are not much help in overcoming the most important initial problem of any self-build society. Some of them are prepared to advance money for construction but this is usually in four stage payments, and only on the value of built work and not on unfixed materials. This can mean serious cash flow problems for the group, particularly if there are delays in the building programme. They will also charge a stage payment valuation fee to each property irrespective of how many houses of the same kind are being inspected during one survey. The Housing Corporation makes no charge and the local authorities usually make only a nominal charge.

8.11 A building society will tend to give a building loan only to those groups whose members agree to finance their house purchase on completion with a mortgage from the same society.

8.12 Banks have only been involved to a small extent with the financing of self-build groups. The terms and conditions of the loan are usually dependant upon the attitude of the branch manager and his knowledge of the individuals within the group. Where loans have been available they have been granted on similar terms to those of the Building Societies, and the interest charges have tended to be very high in comparison with the other lending agencies.

8.13 Usually most building societies will consider applications from self-builders for mortgages on their completed houses. Members should make an application in principle, if possible, as soon as the scheme is under way. Because the final market value will be upwards of 20 per cent more than the cost of the property, this difference being the amount of the member's labour, it is not unusual for societies to make 95 or 100 per cent mortgages available. However, it is important that the group relate their estimated costs of the houses at the beginning of the scheme to the members' incomes, otherwise there will be difficulty negotiating the individual mortgages. Also building societies will normally give preference to regular savers with the society.

8.14 Option mortgage subsidy is available to approved self-build societies.[41] Individual members may obtain either tax relief on their interest payments or opt for subsidy when they buy their houses, provided in either case that it is their only or main residence and the loan does not exceed £25,000.

9. THE FORMATION AND ORGANISATION OF HOUSING CO-OPERATIVES

9.1 Unlike many other countries, there is no legal, administrative and financing system in Britain designed to support co-operative housing[42] In 1974 the Minister for Housing and Construction convened a working party on housing co-operatives because the Government believed that the development of co-operative housing was essential to a sound social and housing policy; its terms of reference were:

> "To report on ways, legislative, financial, and administrative, by which Government, local government, housing associations, the house building industry, and financial and other institutions can enable the formation of housing co-operatives to take place; on ways in which local authority and housing association tenants can be enabled by co-operative management schemes to participate collectively in decisions which affect them; on ways in which tenants may by means of housing co-operatives acquire a financial stake in their homes, and on ways in which the current problem of co-ownership can be tackled".

9.2 In its published report[43] the Working Party took the view that only non-equity co-operatives, in which tenant members collectively own or lease the property but have either no individual stake in the equity or a stake limited to a share repayable on leaving at its original "par" value, were co-operatives in the full sense of the word. It is this type of housing co-operative that we are concerned with here.

9.3 Housing co-operatives of this type are constituted and organised on the principles agreed by the International Co-operative Alliance[44] which are summarised as follows:

(i) Open and voluntary membership.

(ii) Democratic organisation — one person, one vote.

(iii) Limited or no interest on capital.

(iv) Equitable distribution of co-operatively earned surplus or savings, decided by the members common amenities for members and co-operative development and education.

(v) Continuous education in co-operative principles and techniques.

(vi) Co-operation among co-operatives.

This means that no member owns an individual house or flat but is an equal shareholder in the Co-operative which owns the whole deve-ment. Unlike tenants in private or public rented property, it gives people the responsibility for making decisions in the framework of a self-governing community based on mutual help rather than private gain or distant bureaucracy.

9.4 Once a group of people have decided that forming themselves into a co-operative would be the most satisfactory way of solving their hous-ing needs they have to make a second basic decision on the type of property they require. According to local conditions, their scheme may be the buying and improving of existing property or the building of new houses or flats. Although most of the points of organisation and finance described here could be applied to the former, it is with new buildings that this book is primarily concerned.[45]

9.5 To qualify for the Government's Housing Association Grant, which will cover most of the development costs, the co-operative must be able to show that the present housing conditions of its members, or those people who have applied to become members, are not satisfactory. The Housing Corporation have provided some guidelines[46] which should be carefully studied as it is doubtful if finance will be forth-coming from any other source at the present time.[47]

9.6 Having established that they satisfy to the criteria,[48] the founder mem-bers of the co-operative must constitute themselves as a legal body in order to borrow money and enter into contracts. This is normally done by registering with the Registrar of Friendly Societies[49] as a non-profit company with limited liability whose membership must be not less than seven.

9.7 At, or before, this stage the founder members will be wise to contact both the National Federation of Housing Associations and the Co-operative Housing Agency.[50] The former for advice on company regis-tration, and possible affiliation[51] and the latter for advice on the opti-mum size of their membership and how they can best achieve their objectives. Both organisations have experienced development staff whose advice will be crucial to a successful outcome of the co-operatives' future plans, if only because of the extremely complex bureaucratic system within which these will have to be carried out.

9.8 The rules under which the co-operative must be constituted have to be acceptable to both the Registrar of Friendly Societies and the Hous-ing Corporation. Such Model Rules have been drawn up by the NFHA and will be the ones referred to here, but the C.H.A. is also prepared to advise and draw up alternatives to these.[52]

9.9 Having successfully registered the co-operative, and elected a management committee and its officers, the next hurdle to be overcome is the finding of a sponsoring body which is able to carry out the initial development of the intended scheme. It is most unlikely that the lending authority will support the scheme without the appointment of experienced professional consultants. It is also unlikely that these consultants will take on such work on a speculative basis.[53] So assuming that the professional skills necessary are not available from amongst the membership, the only sponsoring organisations acceptable to the Housing Corporation at the present time are either a Secondary Housing Co-operative or a Housing Association, and both of these must be registered with the Corporation.

9.10 Always providing that they consider the co-operative's ideas to be viable, these servicing agencies[54] are able to carry out the work on a speculative basis and will help the co-operative to find land; negotiate with the local authority for planning permissions; discuss designs and costs with the Department of the Environment; and apply to the Housing Corporation for finance.[55]

9.11 As soon as it can the co-operative should decide on its objectives, goals and policies, and set up an organisational structure to achieve these. It is important for the members to understand that they must be responsible for all decisions, and not become dependent upon a servicing agency, as it is they who are the eventual owner-builders. The Director of the Co-operative Housing Agency has already expressed concern that the control of housing co-operatives can so easily be taken over by the people who help them to get started, and that it is in the best interests of the eventual tenant members for them to learn the skills of management control as soon as possible. His report is essential reading for an understanding of some of the pitfalls which can beset the control of a co-operative development in its early stages.[56]

9.12 It is not the purpose here to set out the details of the appropriate organisational and management structures, these are well described in the Model Rules and the publications of the National Federation of Housing Associations and the Co-operative Housing Agency.[57] Once the Co-operative has decided how its members can best be involved there is one further step it must take, followed by a series of important decisions.

9.13 Having worked with its professional consultants on the design of the housing scheme, to the point where all the members are assured that it will satisfy their needs, the co-operative must now apply to the Housing Corporation for registration as a Housing Association.[58] Until this registration is approved, the co-operative will not become eligible for Housing Association Grant nor be given authorisation to acquire land and proceed with a detailed design and costing of the scheme.[59]

9.14 The design specification and estimated cost of the scheme will have to be agreed with the Department of the Environment to conform to their standards and cost yardstick. Once the Department's approval has been received, the Housing Corporation will issue authority to proceed with the documents necessary for tendering. Selective competitive tendering for the contract will be the normal method and the co-operative and its consultants should ensure that only those contractors in whom they have confidence as to both technical performance and financial stability are selected for the tender list.[60]

9.15 The decision to accept the tender will be the co-operative's, following which they will have to seek the approval of the lending authority and the Department of the Environment to enter into a contract with the selected builder. All contractual obligations will rest on the members of the co-operative and therefore it is important that they have experienced legal advice available.

9.16 Once the contract is let and building starts, the whole operation will come under the control of the co-operative's consultant architect. He will be in sole charge of the site and will certify all stage payments due to the contractors. The co-operative will then be responsible for payment using the money received from the lending authority. On completion, the co-operative will be entirely responsible for the buildings handed over to it.

9.17 During the time the houses are being built the co-operative will have to make decisions on the management procedures it will adopt; on the allocation of dwellings and tenancy agreements; on the criteria which will be used for the choosing of new members; on general administration and the method of rent collection; on the organisation of repairs and maintenance; on an educational programme, and ways in which members can be informed of what is going on both within the co-operative and in the co-operative housing movement outside.

In addition annual accounts have to be prepared for submission to both the Registrar of Friendly Societies Societies and the Housing

Corporation, the decision to appoint an auditor and seek advice on the most appropriate accounting system will have to be taken at an early stage.

9.18 Finally the co-operative will have to decide whether its members can do all, or part, of these tasks on a voluntary basis, or whether it will employ somebody or agency to do them. Obviously the more money it can save out of its management and maintenance allowances[61] the more it will create surplus to spend on other purposes and amenities. Whatever it decides, the co-operative must ensure that it is firmly in control of all these matters at all times, and that all decisions are made collectively.

10.   FINANCE FOR HOUSING CO-OPERATIVES

10.1 At the present time it seems unlikely that housing co-operatives will be able to finance their schemes other than through government funds.[62] The public lending authority is either the local council or the regional office of the Housing Corporation and the finance is made available in two stages. Stage 1 is Loan Finance[63] to cover the capital costs of the approved project, these are: the acquisition of the land and related legal fees; the cost of building with related professional fees; and acquisition and development allowances accruing to the co-operative.[64]

10.2 Stage 2 is when the scheme is complete; at which time the total development cost is split into two parts. One part becomes a mortgage loan which is paid by the co-operative, over 60 years in the case of newly built property. The amount of the mortgage loan which the co-operative can afford to repay is calculated on the amount of rent income it will receive from its members. These rents are 'fair rents' fixed by the Rent Officer.

10.3 The second part of the cost, which is often over three quarters of the total, is paid to the lending authority by the Government as a grant known as the Housing Association Grant (HAG). So the co-operative usually ends up by repaying less than a quarter of the cost of developing the property it owns.

10.4 The calculation and payment of Housing Association Grant is determined by Department of the Environment Circulars which are updated from time to time. Besides covering the deficit arising on the capital cost of the project HAG also covers allowances to meet day-to-day outgoings on management and maintenance incurred by the co-operative. It is out of these allowances that the co-operative must also provide for cyclical maintenance, such as outside painting.

10.5 A further grant, the Revenue Deficit Grant, is available to the co-operative if it incurs a deficit on its annual revenue account in any separate accounting year.[65] This is a discretionary grant and will be paid to the co-operative only after a careful scrutiny of expenditure and income.

10.6 Consideration is being given by Government to the case for making rent allowances available to tenants of non-equity co-operatives registered under the Industrial and Provident Societies Act 1965 where the rules provide for full mutuality of tenants and members.[66] Under the present legislation, full mutuality does not qualify for these allowances.

10.7 Because the Government belives that education in co-operative principles and practice is vital to the success of co-operative housing, the Housing Corporation supplies the Co-operative Housing Agency with limited funds to make grants for educational programmes. To qualify for grant the co-operative would have to consult with the CHA Education Officer on the design of an acceptable programme.

10.8 When the founder members first come together they will need money to register the co-operative and buy membership certificates and a seai. They will also need money for postage and telephone calls, and general office expenses, all of which can amount to around £150. So it is important to realise at the start that raising funds to cover these expenses is a task the membership will have to take on before they can proceed to the first stage of their development.

11. THE ROLE OF THE DESIGNER

11.1 In the last few years the British public has been made aware of the many failures in house design and the architectural profession has come in for a great deal of criticism, some of it justified and some not. Through television and the press, concern has been expressed both about the technical failures that have occurred and about the failure of housing to satisfy people's special and social needs, particularly in the local authority sector. Many of the reasons for these failures have been extensively covered by critics of both the present system of housing provision in this country and the professionals involved.

It is not the purpose of this Chapter to enlarge on the ever-increasing volume of this critical appraisal, but in the context of owner-built housing the following quotation at least is appropriate. "The certified professional makes a fool of himself and often does a great deal of harm to other people, by assuming that he knows more than the "uneducated" by virtue of his schooling. All that second and third-hand information and intellectual exercising does for him, however, is to reduce his ability to listen and learn about situations significantly different from his own social and economic experience — with consequences which can be tragic when he has the power to impose his solutions on those who are not strong enough to resist." [67]

11.2 Those designers who have become aware of these short-comings, and they are relatively few in number, have tried to assume two main roles. The first being one of experimenter, in which they have researched and developed methods of design and construction aimed at giving unskilled people the chance to build easily and quickly. The second, and probably more important one, is that of a professional servant in a learning situation with user clients; described by Hans Harms as the co-operative developmental model of working relations and decision-making:

> "This model is based on mutual trust and radical democratic principles rather than on authority by status or credentials. To implement the model in architectural and community planning work, mutual trust has to be developed on the basis of legally binding contractual relations, on mutual loyalties and appreciations, and on mutual goals toward social change, with the understanding that both have to give and take." [68]

11.3 It is difficult for designers to carry out experiments on the appropriate techniques for self-builders; for who is willing to pay for these and who is willing to be experimented upon? So most of the ideas have remained in the realm of theory, and the practical examples are few in number. The two houses shown in Appendix B are both examples of the outcome of patient research into and developments of simple methods of construction which can be used by unskilled people, and were designed to give a maximum of flexibility of plan which the user can change at any time.

11.4 In both cases the components are simple, light in weight, and interchangeable; the system of construction easy to understand and capable of fast erection — both houses were built in less than six months; and the finishes easy to maintain. The main material was timber, by far the easiest material for unskilled people to use, and the costs considerably lower than comparable houses using conventional "wet" bricks and mortar construction."

11.5 However, there is no reason why a combination of "dry" and "wet" construction should not be used in accordance with the skills available in the self-build group, and some designers have achieved this successfully. The most important thing being to "rationalise" the method in such a way that it is capable of use with the minimum of time and effort.[69]

A recent report [70] by the Department of the Environment based on information collected from individuals and organisations involved in self-build housing in England and Wales, has shown a need for further investigation into the development of "building kits". These could be a combination of readily available materials, designed in kit form, rather than the factory produced packages whose components the report found to be large and difficult to handle as well as expensive.

But whatever the designer has to offer owner-builders from his experience his schemes will have little meaning for them if they are an imposed solution. An understanding of what the user's real needs are must be an essential part of the designer's function, and this understanding can only be arrived at by the establishment of mutual trust and a true involvement by the user in the design process. This may mean a much longer time for the design to take shape, as it did in the Swindon case studies, but the responsibility for the final decisions will have been a collective one.

12. USER CONTROL OVER THE DESIGN BRIEF

12.1 In the three Swindon cases control over the design brief was established, long before an architect was appointed, by discussions that led to policies which the groups wanted to follow. These in turn set out an 'outline brief' or general direction in which the architect was required to work. These examples show how important it is to decide what the basic requirements are and to set these out in clear terms so that all the members are involved at the outset and understand what they will ask their consultants to do for them.

12.2 A policy statement should set out what kind of accommodation the group hopes to build; what it can afford to pay; what skills are available in the group and how it intends to use them; in what locality the site will be sought and how much support there is for a proposed scheme from the local authority; under what rules the association will be constituted and where it will seek finance. Only when these matters have been decided in general terms can a group begin to make the choice of a design consultant, and give instructions with some confidence. Initial advice on any of the above points can be obtained from the agencies mentioned in the previous chapters at little or no cost.

12.3 Any new build scheme will generally require the appointment of a registered architect to design the houses, obtain planning permission, and certify the work for payment. Advice on the appointment of an architectural consultant, and a description of the services and costs, are contained in the two Manuals previously mentioned.[71]

Although the SCD Manual is for housing co-operatives in a specific category most of the extensive information contained within it is of use to all co-operatives, and some of it would be useful to self-build groups also.

12.4 There are several basic points contained within the SCD Design Manual which are important for both self-build groups and housing co-operatives to note, and which are worth stressing here.

    (i)   Having chosen and appointed their architect, the group should present and discuss their outline brief so that a first design report can be prepared by the consultant;

    (ii) This report should present different ways in which the housing may be laid out on the site chosen; different patterns of access

(iii) Once the site is bought, and the architect is producing sketch designs, the group should re-assess and finalise its policy and objectives to include the specific requirements of the internal house plans and the necessary service equipment. After this stage a cost plan can be prepared, and the architect can finalise the design in accordance with building and planning regulations.

Only by following procedures along these lines can a group hope to achieve both a co-operative work relationship with its consultant and a completed scheme in which the major decisions have been made by the member-users.

13.   DESIGN IN RELATION TO COST

13.1 At the sketch design stage, and when a group is making decisions on specific requirements, the cost element becomes a critical factor in the design process. It is at this point that the architect, or his quantity surveyor, will have to prepare a cost plan to justify the economy of the proposed design.

13.2 In the case of a self-build scheme the design can affect the cost in the following ways:

(i) The choice of the construction method will affect the time taken to build, which in turn will affect the amount of interest paid on the money borrowed for land and materials.

(ii) The standards of interior space, quality of materials and workmanship, and fixed equipment are all variable within certain limits. The building regulations will restrict these to an acceptable minimum, but anything further than this will demand a design specification tailored to costs that members can afford.

(iii) The specification of materials readily available locally at competitive prices, easy to handle and store on site, and not subject to quick deterioration or easy theft will mean that the group is able to organise their site in the most efficient and economical way.

(iv) The detailing of the materials so that the minimum of labour and equipment is required to trim and join them together is essential. Both the size of the materials and the tools used should be as small as practicable to effect the most economies.

(v) The design of the site layout will be determined to a large extent by the local planning regulations, particularly with regard to access and car parking. But the members will have to decide how much garden space and common landscaping they can afford to make the best use of the land. This decision should be determined by a design which needs the minimum of expensive site works.

(vi) The choice of a minimum number of house types, preferably only a different plan within the same 'shell', will mean less design costs, and a standardisation of materials scheduling with resulting economies. Changes and extras after the design has been finalised can only mean increases in final costs, as was the case with Downsview.

13.3 Housing co-operatives, because in most cases they are financed by government lending agencies, will have their costs strictly controlled, and the design will have to accord with a 'cost yardstick'. Cost yard-sticks are published by the Department of the Environment in the form of tables which set the theoretical limit on the amount of money available for housing of a certain standard and quality.

13.4 The effect of these restrictions on the design is considerable as the finance allowed depends on certain conditions: the average number of people per dwelling; the density of dwellings on the site; and the site and road layout. The designer's task is made more difficult by different interpretations of the yardsticks by DoE officers, and by regional variations.

13.5 The procedure adopted goes something like this:

(i)   The District Valuer gives a report and an informal valuation of the cost of the land. Local outline planning approval for the scheme 'in principle' must be received.

(ii) Housing Corporation design requirements must be adhered to if the Corporation is financing the scheme.

(iii) When the co-operative has cleared these two hurdles their design consultant can enter into informal discussions with the DoE regional office on the scheme's acceptability for cost yard-stick. The cost plan, or draft bill of quantities, is prepared by the quantity surveyor and submitted for scrutiny by the DoE.

13.6 At this stage it is more than likely that the co-operative will have to amend its scheme for the cost to be acceptable, very rarely do the first sketch designs seem to come within the limits. So a designer's know-ledge and experience of the cost yardstick requirements are an impor-tant asset, and his ability to negotiate an essential skill.

13.7 To further complicate matters there are certain additional cost allow-ances known as 'ad hocs'; these are for special cases such as expensive foundations due to difficult site conditions, or expensive materials required by a planning authority. Again, the consultant has to make out a case for the additional cost and negotiate with the DoE for approval.

13.8 Having satisfied the DoE that the scheme will come within cost limits the design can be detailed and bills of quantities prepared for tendering. At this stage it is to be hoped that the Quantity Surveyor has made sure that the cost plan is in line with current building costs and that the lowest tender received comes within the cost yardstick. If not, then the co-operative is faced with some very difficult decisions affecting the very nature of their scheme. Housing Association Grant is still available provided the limit is not exceeded by 10% and the design does not include uneconomic features and too high standards. But the viability of the scheme and the ability of the consultants could be in doubt as government demands value for money. It is a situation many co-operatives have found themselves faced with, a situation which has threatened the design of the scheme they had set their hearts on building.

ADVISORY AND SERVICING AGENCIES

14. GOVERNMENT AGENCIES

14.1 The Housing Corporation[72] has the statutory duty to promote and assist in self build societies, and the ways in which it can do this are set out in the DoE Circular 118/75.

14.2 The Housing Corporation is also responsible for promoting and advising on co-operative housing. This is done through its Co-operative Housing Agency[73] which performs four basic functions:

(i) Creating a suitable legislative and administrative framework for housing co-operatives;

(ii) Helping to make available financial resources for co-operative development;

(iii) Promoting the principles and techniques of co-operative housing nationally;

(iv) Providing assistance in legal, financial, educational, project development and housing management matters to co-operatives and development groups.

14.3 During its short life, the Agency has carried out an ambitious and active programme despite the lack of adequate financial resources. Through its Advisory Committee it has made recommendations to the Government on the need for new legislation for housing co-operatives, and is at present producing a Handbook which aims to show co-operatives what choices they have under the existing legislation.

14.4 It has had only limited success in helping co-operatives to receive the financial resources they need for development. As the previous chapters have shown, these are tightly controlled by the Housing Corporation, and by central and local government departments, and little or no power has been devolved to the Agency for their allocation. It can only advise on how co-operatives might find access to these resources.

14.5 Its support for the formation of co-operatives, however, has been considerable, particularly in project development, legal advice, and educational materials. The Directory[75] recently published shows an increase in total members housed from 1850 in April 1977 to 5,430 in June 1978, an achievement for which some of the credit must go to the staff of the Agency.

14.6 Despite this there is still much criticism of its "official" status. The view of the Working Party on Co-operative Housing on the Agency's future was that it should eventually become a body democratically controlled by the members of the housing co-operative movement and acting on their behalf. But in the words of one member of its present Advisory Committee "the vision . . . is still only a mirage".[76]

14.7 The National Building Agency was set up in 1964, by the Minister of Public Building and Works, as a grant aided non-profit limited company to give advice and professional help to the construction industry and its clients with the object of improving building methods and techniques. About twenty per cent of the Agency's activities are promoted by grant, the rest being paid for by consultancy service fees. Since the early 1970's its technical consultancy services have been available to housing associations and self-build groups, though its overall contribution has been relatively small since then. Probably because of its commitment to large-scale industrialised building methods during the 1960's it may now be having difficulty convincing potential clients that its experience is relevant to small-scale, local user-controlled construction.

The fee scale is similar to that of the building professionals in private practice. Initial advice to self build groups has been provided free of charge under the Agency's grand aid.

14.8 Local Authorities have in some cases helped self-build groups to form, and continued to give them advice as their schemes develop. They have also given support to housing co-operatives in a few cases and it is hoped that this involvement will continue to grow, as long as the services are not offered in a "paternalistic" way and with "bureaucratic" strings attached.

15.   SELF-BUILD MANAGEMENT

15.1 There are a very small number of professional management consultants operating in Britain who offer their services to self-build groups, and it would be fair to say at this time that an even smaller number have both the qualified staff and proper experience to back up the kind of services self-builders may require from them.

15.2 The services offered by these consultants can vary considerably but usually include: initial advice on the setting up of the group; finding the land and arranging finance; and advice on design, estimating and site management. The group must decide for themselves which of these services they require and ensure that a detailed contract is drawn up. The fees can vary considerably but will almost certainly be between 3% and 9% of the total development cost. There is an increasing body of opinion that believes an extension of this kind of service is now urgent if self-build is to make any significant contribution to an increased choice of housing.

16.   SECONDARY CO-OPERATIVES AND HOUSING ASSOCIATIONS

16.1 One way for co-operatives, either established or in the development stage, to gain the services they need is to form a federation of groups which could then afford to employ the staff to provide these services. These would consist of development assistance; design and management skills; and information and educational facilities which could be shared. In this case the groups would be known as 'primary' co-operatives and the federation as a 'secondary' co-operative, the whole being democratically controlled by the membership.

16.2 As the N.F.H.A. has rightly pointed out, there is a fundamental problem here: "It is the "chicken and egg" situation. There are not very many housing co-ops in existence and certainly very few areas where there are several in a locality. Thus, until more primary co-ops exist, it is hard to support the establishment of secondary co-ops. Conversely, until there are secondary co-ops to service them, primary co-ops are unlikely to develop (unless they use a housing association as a service agency).[77] That was written in the early part of 1976 and since then no satisfactory way around that situation has been found.

16.3 Out of the secondary co-operatives which have been formed[78] none can be called federated bodies democratically controlled by their members. But despite many criticisms of their lack of democracy they have performed an important development function, and without them many housing co-operatives would have failed to get their schemes approved and built.

In the future it will be up to the primary groups, acting together, to push hard for help and resources from the Housing Corporation to be made available for the formation of secondary co-operatives which are truly democratic and capable of giving services in ways which accord to the co-operative principles.

16.4 At present the only alternative to the forming of secondary co-operatives is the use of existing Housing Associations. They are acceptable to the Housing Corporation and they have practical experience in project development and property management.

But Housing Associations are set up as non-profit landlords and do not subscribe to the co-operative principles; so that appart from a few exceptions they do not know how co-operatives work nor do they understand their members' needs. A co-operative would simply be buying the services they offer and would not be sharing control of the organisation as they would be in the case of the secondary co-operatives.

16.5 The services of a Housing Association would also demand most of the allowances accruing to the co-operative.[79] Certainly at the development stage all the allowances would be required by this type of servicing agency; and after occupation a fairly long term management contract would almost certainly be required. So any advantages the co-operative could gain by using the allowances efficiently itself would be lost for quite some time, as well as a measure of control and a chance to learn management skills by doing the job itself.

17. FEDERATIONS AND LIBRARIES

17.1 There are two national federations giving support and advice to self-build groups and housing co-operatives; the National Federation of Housing Associations and the Federation of Co-operatives. There is also a national resource centre; the Self-Help Housing Resource Library at the Polytechnic of North London.

17.2 The NFHA was set up in 1935 to provide a national voice for housing societies in Britain. Although it is mainly concerned with matters dealing with Housing Associations, in recent years it has been helping both self-build societies and housing co-operatives and has staff working in both fields. It has produced two manuals: the Co-operative Housing Handbook; and a manual for Self-Build Housing Associations together with the National Building Agency and the Housing Corporation. Both are essential reading to intending self-builders and co-operators.[80] The services of the Federation are extended to those groups who affiliate on an annual subscription basis.

17.3 In the report of the Working Party on Housing Co-operatives there were some tentative suggestions put forward that co-operatives' members should be represented at the national level by a federated body democratically elected. In 1976 several members of existing co-operatives throughout the country decided to take the initiative and form the nucleus of such a federation.

17.4 After a series of meetings, and a great deal of argument, a constitution was finally agreed and the Federation of Housing Co-operatives was registered in February 1977. It has had some trouble convincing the Government and the Housing Corporation that it speaks as a representative body of the co-operative housing movement but with financial aid from the National Consumer Council it has now gained a regional membership and later this year it is hoping to increase and strengthen this membership through a number of meetings and workshops held throughout the country. It is open for affiliation by any housing co-operative group.

17.5 The Self-Help Housing Resource Library[81] was set up in 1977 with a grant from the Gulbenkian Foundation and has two basic aims in mind:

(i) To assist in the collection and flow of information about self-help approaches to the housing problem.

(ii)   To give aid to the development of self-help alternatives wherever possible.

The library is for use by anyone, and although certain material is available for loan most of it is for reference only.

17.6 The Library is also acting as a centre for several research and field work projects, and provides lecturing facilities and a newsletter. It is to be hoped that its example will be followed by other similar iniatives on a local or regional basis.

SUMMARY

The following is a brief summary of do's and don'ts learned from the case studies, and from experience gained with other groups and their schemes. This is not an exhaustive list, and initial advice should be taken, wherever possible, from people who are knowledgeable in the field of self-held housing to avoid the many pitfalls which have caused so much frustration to enthusiastic and well-intentioned people throughout the country.[82]

18.   FOR SELF-BUILD GROUPS

18.1   Keep the first group small — you only need seven members to register — and then choose and add members after careful selection. Ask for a reasonable membership down payment and weekly subscription, but high enough to test the seriousness of the applicant. Don't recruit until you are sure of purchasing the land and have decided on the type and number of houses. Finding land is going to be your most difficult problem, even so don't just take the first piece that comes along, make sure it's suitable and worth the price.

18.2   Decide on the house design and method of construction according to the available skills within the membership. Don't appoint an architect until you have decided your policy and 'outline' brief. Choose an experienced and sympathetic consultant; don't use a consultant who does not understand the needs of self-builders.

Consider the use of 'kits', or a simple and fast construction method; be guided by your architect on this. Don't attempt a construction method which will tax your skills.

Try to make use of all members of the family; don't allow the opinions of other groups to put you off using the resources of all the people you have available.

Remember the final design must be one all the members can afford.

18.3   Establish good relationships with the local authority; they may be able to find a site, and should be able to advance the loan for building. But they will want to be sure that you are well organised and have the right kind of professional advice before they give you support. Try to gain the confidence of the senior officers and committee chairmen, if you gain their support there is a good chance that there will be fewer delays caused by the more junior bureaucrats.

18.4   Choosing the lending agency for the building loan carefully. Shop around to find the best interest rates and the most favourable stage payments. Try to get the interest payments capitalised so that members do not have to find these out of their subscriptions. Make sure the stage claims are efficiently compiled and checked with the Architect for his certification thus ensuring quick payment and good cash flow.

18.5   Register with the Registrar of Friendly Societies as soon as you know the land is available. You will need the limited liability of the registration before you make any contracts. Don't use the NFHA for registration if you don't want to, but this will probably be the quickest and easiest way even if it does cost you more money.

18.6 Start negotiations with Building Societies for individual members' mortgages as soon as possible. Don't start a scheme which the members cannot afford to finance out of their incomes.

18.7 Choose your solicitor and accountant on the basis of their understanding of your needs. Decide if you require a servicing agency to help with the management of the scheme. Don't agree a contract of engagement with any consultants without knowing exactly what services they are going to provide.

18.8 Adopt rules which are suitable for the membership and, if necessary, draw up a working agreement. Do not proceed with the scheme until these are fully understood and agreed by all the members.

Work out specific jobs for all the members and don't start building until these have been agreed by all the members.

Don't allocate houses until after the first completions, otherwise members will tend to concentrate most effort on their own houses.

Don't allow "extras" until after completion unless they are carefully budgeted into the cost and do not affect the work programme unduly.

18.9 Choose and buy plant, equipment and tools carefully. Don't buy large expensive equipment which needs expensive servicing and may have a poor re-sale value. Hiring may be considered for some plant or equipment but will probably be uneconomic because of the "standing" time during the weekdays. Some plant hirers might make a special rate however.

18.10 Keep sub-contract work to a minimum; contract good and reliable tradesmen even if their cost may be on the high side. Don't award a contract without getting competitive prices.

18.11 Set up an efficient materials buying and accounting system. Don't buy any more materials than you need for the work programme as this can affect the amount of interest charges on the building loan. However, you will have to estimate whether the lower prices and discounts on bulk buying offset this charge favourably. Make sure you register for VAT, and get the most competitive prices and discounts.

18.12 On winding-up, make sure that there is an exact costing of each house with a correct estimate of outstanding loans and charges. Don't forget to add a generous reserve to cover any bills or charges that have accrued at the time of winding up.

19. FOR HOUSING CO-OPERATIVES

19.1 Before deciding to set up a co-operative, talk to people in existing housing co-ops and ask to attend their meetings. Try to read as much about the subject as you can taking particular note of the CHA Outlines, and have a good understanding of the co-operative principles before deciding this could be the best way of solving your housing needs.

Keep the original group to about seven members — the minimum legally allowed — and don't recruit members until you are quite sure what is involved in getting a co-operative started.

19.2 Check on the critieria laid down by the Housing Corporation to see if your housing needs come within its terms of reference for government financing; it is unlikely that you will get financial help from any other source at the present time. If you qualify then don't approach any government agency until you have decided an outline policy which states your aims, what kind of houses you would like to build and approximately what size you think the eventual co-operative membership should be.

19.3 Discuss your aims and objectives with the CHA to find out what are the chances of support from the Housing Corporation. Make contact with those members and officers of your local authority who may have some sympathy with your aims, you are going to need a lot of support from them to achieve these, and you may even persuade them to supply the loan finance. Don't go too far with your organisation and scheme before you have had discussions with these two bodies or you may suffer many disappointments. Check the CHA Outlines carefully.

19.4 Check with the NFHA and CHA on rules and registration. The CHA may be able to recommend rules which suit you better than the NFHA model rules. Don't spend money on the registration with the Registrar of Friendly Societies until you have been advised by the CHA that your co-operative scheme also has a chance of being registered by the Housing Corporation. If you think your chances are good then decide on ways and means to raise the £150 you will need for the first registration and to cover general administrative expenses.

19.5 You will probably have to persuade a Secondary Co-operative or Housing Association to sponsor your scheme and do the initial development work on a speculative basis, if so them make sure they fully understand what *you* want and don't let them dictate policy.

19.6 Prepare your outline design 'brief' carefully so that when you appoint an architect he has clear instructions on what your requirements are. Don't allow your consultants to make decisions for you unless you have instructed him to do this. He should be giving you the benefit of his experience so use his services in the most effective way, but don't lose your control of the development. Use the SCD Design Manual for guidance.

19.7 Choose your consultants carefully giving preference to those who have either already worked with co-operatives of who fully understand the co-operative principles. Don't make any formal contractual agreements with consultants until you are sure your scheme will get approval. Make sure your architect fully understands the constraints of the cost yardsticks.

19.8 Before signing a contract with a servicing agency decide what development, management and maintenance work can be carried out by your members. Don't sign a long-term contract, you may find that you can learn the skills and do the work yourselves quite soon.

19.9 Make sure you have a firm but flexible policy on the procedure for recruiting new members. Don't conduct interviews without stating quite clearly what you expect from new members and what you have to offer them.

19.10 Make sure you have a policy and programme on information sharing and education which encourages all members to participate. Don't allow a state of affairs in which the co-operative depends on a few knowledgeable members to run the show, or depends on a servicing agency to do all the work.

19.11 Keep in touch with other co-operatives and learn from their successes and mistakes. Don't allow your co-op to become isolated from the rest of the housing co-operative movement. Try to keep people in your locality informed about what you are attempting to do. There is a lot of misunderstanding by local people and local authorities about the housing co-operative movement, don't encourage this by keeping apart from the local community.

APPENDIX A

Downsview Self-Build Housing Association

Twelve two-storey detached family houses sited around a cul-de-sac, with gardens and integral single-car garages.

Floor area 1,200 sq. ft.   Total site area 1.382 acres
Garage   128 sq. ft.

Specification

Foundations: Concrete strip foundations in trenches to exterior load-bearing walls.

Walls: Exterior load-bearing walls to carry the roof in 4½" heather-coloured facing bricks, 2" cavity, 4" thermalite blocks to interior plastered face.

                 Internal ground floor partitions in 4" termalite blocks with plastered face.

                 Internal first floor partitions in 3" x 2" timber studding with plasterboard and skim both sides. Chimney stack in random stone with flue-liner.

                 All windows and doors in timber with the exception of an exterior sliding aluminium patio door to dining area.

Roof: Standard gang-nailed trusses with concrete interlocking tiles on timber battens on reinforced roofing felt, finished with timber verge. 3" glass fibre quilt in roof void.

Floors: Ground floor 4" concrete slab on hardcore, 2000 grade polythene waterproof sheet on top of slab, finished with ½" concrete screed to receive thermoplastic tiles. First floor 1" flooring grade chipboard on 7" x 2" timber joists. Staircase in timber.

Ceilings: $\frac{3}{8}$" plaster board and skim.

Heating: Small-bore water system with radiators and gas-fired boiler. Fireplace in lounge.

Estimated Costs:

Estimated cost per house prepared by the Architect in March 1976:

	£
Materials	6,275
Sub-contract work	735
Electrical, telephone and water services	220
Plant and tools	213
Fees: Architect, Solicitor, accountant and valuer	334
Insurances	45
Land and legal fees	3,800
TOTAL	£11,622

Note: The total cost of the house is likely to be about £12,100 including interest charges on completion in mid-1978.

It must also be pointed out that considerable savings were made, estimated at over £1,000 per house, by buying materials during 1975/76 when the group was waiting for its site. However, this is a risk many groups may not be prepared to take with their personal finances.

The following is a schedule showing the anticipated quarterly loan requirements. the figures here are provisional and the eventual claims were based on actual expenditure as the work proceeded, thus having an effect on the cost of interest charged on the borrowing.

	1st Quarter £	1st Quarter £	1st Quarter £	1st Quarter £
Site purchase	42,000.00			
Legal Fees	3,600.00			500.00
Valuer's Fees	60.93			
Architect's Fees	1,950.00			1,050.00
Accountant's Fees				500.00
Insurances	490.00			
Sub Contractors	3,675.00	5,145.00		
Plant	1,000.00	1,250.00		
Tools	150.00	50.00	50.00	50.00
Services			540.00	2,080.00
Paths, Verges and Fences				4,851.72
Building Materials	17,815.75	20,989.40	20,895.75	10,755.75
Quarterly Totals	£70,841.68	27,434,40	21,485.75	19,787.47

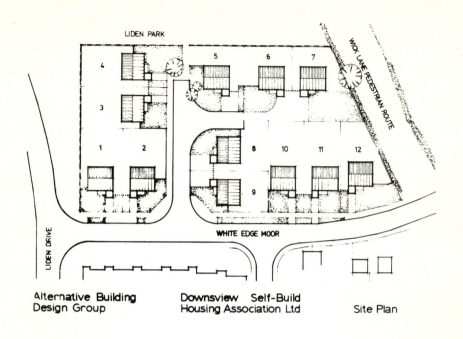

Alternative Building
Design Group

Downsview Self-Build
Housing Association Ltd

Site Plan

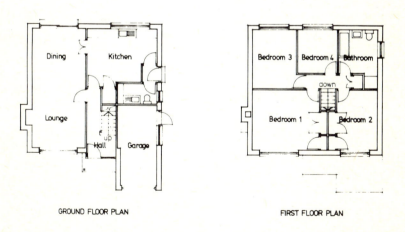

GROUND FLOOR PLAN

FIRST FLOOR PLAN

Alternative Building
Design Group

Downsview Self-Build
Housing Association Ltd

Plans

Downsview houses with members working on site.

Toothill Self-Build Housing Association

Eleven single storey detached family houses sited around a cul-de-sac, with gardens and car parking spaces (no garages).
Floor area 1,004 sq. ft.   Total site area 1.335 acres

Specification:

Foundations: 2'0" x 2'0" concrete piers Hand dug to a depth of 3'0".

Frame: Post and beam construction with filler joists using stress-graded timber.
Columns 2" x 6" high grade timber
Beams   2" x 8"   "   "   "
Floor and roof filler joists
2" x 8" lower grade timber.
This is a calculated frame with joints bolted together with galvanised bolts.

Roof: 2" wood wool slabs on wood joists covered with 3 layers of bituminous felt with lower layer loose on the slabs. Finish ¾" clean loose gravel ballast 1½" in depth.

Walls: Exterior: Outer face, coloured Glasal Sheets;
2" wood wool slab;
inner face ½" plaster board.
Interior: 2" wood wool slabs with ½" plasterboard on both sides. Finish can either be natural or paint or wallpaper.
Kitchen and bathroom walls have plastic finished board in place of plasterboard.

Note: All walls are held in positions by battens, the fitting is by friction (no nailing or screwing) to allow for easy removal and refixing giving maximum flexibility for change.

Floors: 6" wide tongued and grooved softwood floorboards, or hardwood long strip flooring, on timber joists. The exterior underside of the floor joists are finished with Eternit on timber battens. The space between the Eternit and floorboards being filled with 3" mineral wood thermal insulation.

Ceilings: ¾ Gyproc plank with vapour check.

Heating: Small- bore water system with radiators and gas-fired boiler.
                    No fireplaces were required by the group.

Estimated Costs

Estimated cost of materials delivered to site per house, prepared by the
Quantity Surveyor at April 1977 prices:

	£
Main Structure	3,952
Kitchen fittings	160
Sanitary fittings; soil, waste and overflow pipes and fittings	240
Hot and cold water and heating materials including boiler, tanks radiators, pipes and fittings	640
Electrical materials including switches, power and lighting points, wiring and conduit as required but excluding light fittings	370
Roofing work to be carried out by a sub-contractor, including materials	396
	£5,758

Additional items per house, estimated by the Toothill group:

Drainage and sewer connection	60
Perimeter fencing	10
Cross-over and public footpaths	28
Electric, Gas and Water connections	114
Plant and tools required, not accounting for re-sale	117
Insurances	41
	£370
Total	£6,128

Estimated cost of Architect's and Quantity Surveyor's fees per house	692
Estimated cost of land per house	2,700
	£3,392

Estimated total cost of house, land and consultant fees	£9,520

Note: This cost does not include solicitors and accountant's fees, and no sub-contract work has been allowed for other than roofing. At this stage the group felt they would like to take on all the building work themselves even though they were not trained in the required skills. The architect's services included the co-ordination of both material supplies and the work on site, but even though the heating, plumbing and elec-

Typical plan of
single storey house

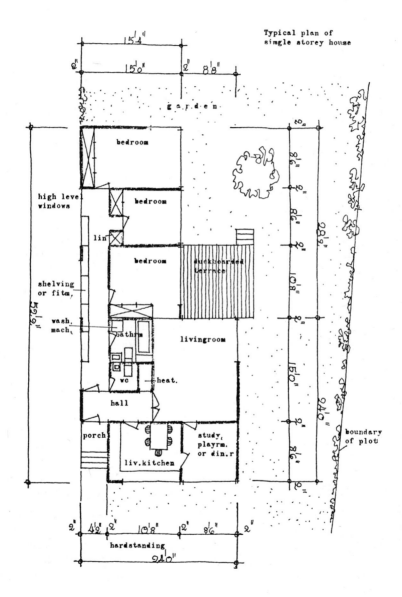

elevations and section
of typical house

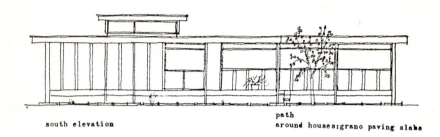

south elevation

path
around houses:grano paving slabs

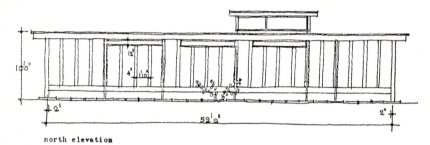

north elevation

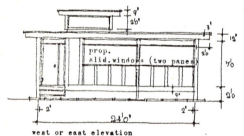

west or east elevation

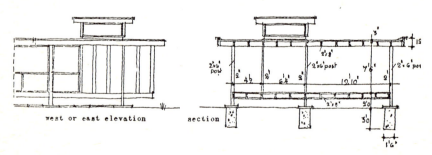

west or east elevation

section

trical systems were simply designed some specialist guidance would have been needed.

Interest charges on the money borrowed for building has to be added to the total cost also. This is related to the time taken to complete and would have been at the rate of about 12% in 1977.

Toothill Co-operative Dwellings

Seventy single-person dwellings, comprising 46 studio-bedroom units and 24 bedsitter units, built in seven semi-circular blocks on a self-contained site with access road, parking spaces and gardens.

Studio units 402 square ft. approx. Total site in area 3.512 acres
Bedsitters   278 square ft. approx. 3.512 acres

Specification

Foundations:	Reinforced concrete slab on hardcore.
Walls:	External 4½" facing brick, 2" cavity, internal face 4" termal block walls with plastered face standard timber windows and doors. Internal walls dividing the units 8" load bearing blocks. Walls within units 4" blockwork. All plastered and finished with emulsion paint.
Roof:	Timber truss structure to bedsitter units; combination timber truss structure with purlins and rafters to studio units. All with concrete interlocking roof tiles on timber battens.
Floors:	Thermoplastic tiles on concrete screed on polythene sheet damp-proof membrane on concrete foundation slab. Studio unit bedrooms timber joists and boards.
Ceilings:	½" plasterboard on timber joists with Autex finish. 3" glass fibre insulation above boards.
Heating:	Space heating in studio units by gas fireplace and flue convector heater; in bedsitters by gas fireplace.
	Water heating by gas-fired boiler placed under kitchen sinks in each unit.

Cooking by gas-fired stove.

Kitchen equipment:
Steel sink and unit; base, wall, and larder storage units.

Estimated costs

The following are estimated costs prepared by the Quantity Surveyor at April 1978 prices. These costs are for the first submitted scheme and must be taken as approximate figures only:

		£
Studio bedrooms per unit	£5,984	
Bedsitters per unit	£4,428	
Total cost of all units		381,505
External building works, drainage etc.		49,636
Site development works, roads planting etc.		47,475
Parking spaces for 84 cars		9,390
TOTAL		£488,306

The cost of the land will probably be comparable with the Toothill self-build scheme i.e. approx. £30,000 per acre.

The fees for architects and quantity surveyors will total approximately £42,000.

No information is available at this time on any other costs, such as legal fees.

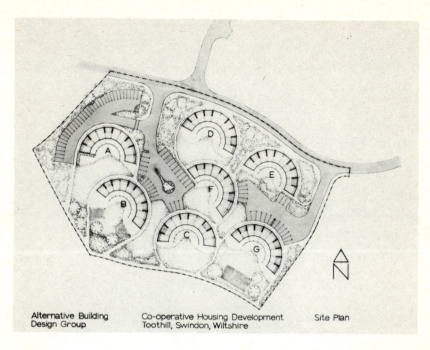

Alternative Building Design Group

Co-operative Housing Development
Toothill, Swindon, Wiltshire

Site Plan

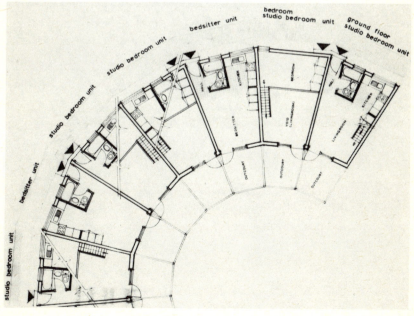

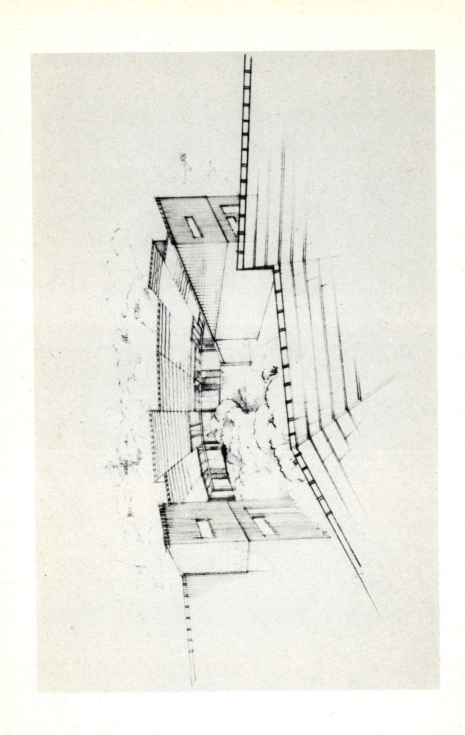

House at Berry Brow, Yorkshire.

House at Bromeswell, Suffolk.

APPENDIX B

Two related houses

House at Berry Brow, Yorkshire
designed by Peter Stead and Robert Clayton

The last in a series of houses built by Peter Stead in the 1950's and 60's to test the use of light easily assembled components, most of them readily obtainable from local suppliers. He built this one for himself in 1969 with the aid of semi-skilled and unskilled labour and completed the work in six months.

The construction method used is: single-storey timber posts, on a concrete slab, carrying a long-beamed flat roof finished with bituminous felt. The slab and the roof were completed first leaving an open flexible space which was then filled in with exterior walls and windows, and interior partitions. These are "dry" materials — timber, asbestos and plasterboard — and can be moved easily if a change of plan is required. The site is a sloping one and therefore added additional costs to the foundation work.

Cost: £3,900 for 1,000 sq. feet, excluding land and site works.

House at Bromeswell, Suffolk

designed by Walter Segal

Built in 1972. This was the second of the self-build houses — the first being in 1966 — to use the timber method Walter Segal has been refining since the early 1960's.

All the work, with the exception of some help with the erection of the frame, was done by the owner and his wife, both schoolteachers with no building skills. They worked in the evening, at weekends, and all their summer holiday, completing the single-storey house without any difficulty in only four months. The drawings were easy to understand, and the parts were in a descriptive manual from which they ordered their materials. The flexibility of the system was amply proved when later they added an extension and simply removed the wall panels and refixed them elsewhere. Again this was done quickly with only six weeks of part-time work.

The specification is similar to the Toothill houses in Appendix A whose appearance would have been much the same.

Cost: £3,195 for 1,000 sq. feet. Extension added in 1974, £982 for 220 sq. feet.

APPENDIX C

REFERENCES

General

1. Housing Acts:

Housing Act 1964
Housing Act 1974
Housing Rents and Subsidies Act 1975

Department of the Environment Circulars:

170/74 — Explains Housing Act 1974
52/75 — Deals with calculation and payment of Housing Association
Grant (HAG).
These are followed by circulars giving updated Administrative
Allowances.
118/75 — Housing Act 1974: Part I Self-Build Societies
8/76 — Housing Co-operatives.

The Acts and Circulars are obtainable from Her Majesty's Stationery
Office, 49 High Holborn, London W.1. There are branches in Edinburgh,
Cardiff, Manchester, Bristol, Birmingham, Belfast.

2. The Housing Corporation, 149 Tottenham Court Road, London W.1.
publications:

—Practice notes for Housing Associations.
—Various Circulars dealing with Housing Association matters, which are
updated from time to time.
—An annual report.
Regional offices are in London, Croydon (Surrey), Potters Bar (Herts),
Cardiff, Exeter, Wolverhampton, Leicester, Manchester, Leeds, Edinburgh.

3. The National Federation of Housing Associations, 30 Southampton
Street, London W.C.2., publications:

—A guide to Housing Associations.
—Co-operative Housing Handbook.
—A Manual for Self-Build Housing Associations (together with the
National Building Agency and the Housing Corporation).
—Housing Management Practices in Housing Associations.

—Housing Act of 1974, relevance to Housing Associations.
—Model Rules for Self-Build Societies.
—Model Rules for Housing Co-operatives.

4. The Registry of Friendly Societies, 17 North Audley Street, London W.1. deals with the registration of Self-Build Societies and Housing Co-operatives as limited liability companies.

5. The National Building Agency, 7 Arundel Street, London W.C.2. gives advice to self-build and housing co-operative groups on technical matters. There are regional offices in Belfast, Cardiff, Edinburgh, Manchester.

6. Self-Help Housing Resource Library, Ladbroke House, Highbury Grove, London N.5. Holds meetings and workshops; produces new letters and reference materials on all aspects of self-help in housing.

7. Books and articles:-

Alice Coleman   *The Use and Misuse of our National Land Resources*
                       Special issue of the Architects Journal, 19 January 1977

John F. C. Turner and Robert Fichter (eds).
                       Freedom to Build
                       The Macmillan Co. New York 1972

John F. C. Turner   *Housing by People*
                       Marion Boyars. London 1976

Stan Windass   *Working Papers on Housing and Land*
                       pub. Foundation for Alternatives, The Rookery, Adderbury, Oxfordshire.

N. J. Habraken   *Supports: An Alternative to Mass Housing*
                       The Architectural Press. London 1972

The following are critical writing on the role of professionals in housing and community development:

Robert Goodman   *After the Planners*
                       Pelican Books. London 1972

Ivan Illich et al   *Disabling Professions*

Marion Boyars. London 1977

Hans Harms   *₊User Involvement: Towards a new professionalism*
The Architects Journal. London 19 January 1977

Conrad Jameson   *Modern Architecture as an ideology*
Architectural Association Quarterly. Vol. 7. No. 4. London Oct/Dec. 1975.

Enter pattern books, exit public housing architects
The Architects Journal. London 11 February 1976

Self-Build

8.   Reports, articles and a book:-

Alternatives in Housing? A report of Self-Build in Britain
Architectural Association. London 1976 obtainable from the AA Bookshop 34—36 Bedford Square, London W.C.1.

Department of the Environment
Self-Build Housing including the use of kits
DoE. Housing Development Directorate. London, 1976 obtainable from Beckett House, 1 Lambeth Palace Road, London S.E.1.

Christine Coleman   *A house for £4,000*
Article in Homes and Gardens September 1975 describing the Segal House at Bromeswell Suffolk (Appendix B)

John Maule McKean   *A certain basic satisfaction in building a shelter for oneself*
Article in the Architects Journal, 3 September 1975, with drawings, photographs and the story of the Segal House at Bromeswell Suffolk (Appendix B).

Colin Wadsworth   *With the right organisation, anyone can build his own house*

A useful brochure and set of leaflets from Colin Wadsworth, Southern House, Hallfield Road, Bradford, Yorkshire.

Stuart Martin   *Build your own house*
A book for the layman which takes the reader through the 'traditional' building process in detail. Published by Stanley Paul & Co., 3 Fitzroy Square, London W.1.

Murray Armor   *Building your own Home*
It is both about and for self-builders and provides a useful source of hard facts for those who are thinking of joining their ranks. Published by Prism Press, Stable Court, Chalmington, Dorchester, Dorset.

Housing Co-operatives

9. The Co-operative Housing Agency, 180 Tottenham Court Road, London W1 9LE, is the first contact point for advice to anyone wishing to set up a housing co-operative.

The CHA publications:

—A regular newsletter CHAT.
—CHA Outlines, a series of leaflets for people who want to develop a housing co-op or organise a co-op education programme.
—Co-operatives and Housing Policy. A report by the CHA Advisory Committee in response to the Government Consultative Document on housing policy (June 1977).
—CHA Directory of Housing Co-operatives 1978. This gives an overall picture of co-operative housing activity in Britain.

10. Federation of Housing Co-operatives, 16 First Cross Road, Twickenham, Middlesex TW2 5QA. Information on housing co-operatives throughout the regions in Britain. Organises regional meetings and workshops.

11. Publications:

Final Report of the Working Party on Housing Co-operatives
Department of the Environment 1975 Published by Her Majesty's Stationery Office.

John Hands	*Housing Co-operatives* published by the Society for Co-operative Dwellings, 209 Clapham Road, London S.W.9.
SCD	*New Build Design Manual for Single People Sharing* published by the Society for Co-operative Dwellings. SCD also publishes a regular newsletter SCOOP.
Manchester Federation of Housing Co-operatives	*How to set up a Housing Co-operative* A well-written and amusing booklet on starting a co-op compiled by housing co-ops in the Manchester area. Can be obtained from Birch Housing Co-op, 9 Slade Lane, Longsight, Manchester 13.
Bertha I. B. Turner	*London Squatters Groups becoming Housing Co-operatives* A study of housing co-operatives forming in the London area in 1977, commissioned by the Building and Social Housing Foundation, Memorial Square, Coalville, Leicestershire.

THE AUTHOR

Peter Stead served his apprenticeship as a mason and bricklayer before becoming a director of his family building firm in 1950. After four years' military service in South East Asia he studied first at Huddersfield College of Technology and later at the University of York and the Architectural Association Graduate School.

In 1963 he went to the U.S.A. as a professor in the School of Architecture at Carnegie Institute of Technology, returning to England in 1966 to continue his building development work. He was Head of the Department of Construction at Huddersfield Technical College for three years before deciding to take up full-time consulting work in 1975, and is now in private practice and a director of AHAS Housing Advisory Services.

He is a qualified Building Surveyor and a Fellow of the Institute of Building.

FOOTNOTES

[1] Begining to test the widely influential hypothesis in Turner's book "Freedom to Build" was a turning point for me:
"When dwellers control the major decisions and are free to make their own contributions in the design, construction, or management of their housing, both this process and the environment produced stimulate individual and social well-being. When people have no control over, nor responsibility for, key decisions in the housing process, dwelling environments may instead become a barrier to personal fulfillment and a burden on the economy.

[2] A charitable organisation formed by Stan Windass in 1972 with a national membership of people concerned to find "alternatives" to the way society was developing in Britain and the rest of the world. Now the Foundation for Alternatives.

[3] Organised by Bertha I. B. Turner in conjunction with the Architectural Association and financed by the Anglo-German Foundation.

[4] Swindon was designated an expanding town in 1953 under the Town Development Act 1952, and was created the Borough of Thamesdown in 1974 under the reorganisation of local government.

[5] These included George McRobie of the Intermediate Technology Development Group; John Hands, Director of the Society for Co-operative Dwellings and now Director of the Co-operative Housing Agency; Colin Wadsworth, Director of a company providing services to self build groups; Charles Cockburn of the co-ownership building firm Sunderlandia Ltd.; and architects Walter Segal and Rod Hackney.

[6] The encouragement we received from Gerald Blythe, the Director of Development & Housing; Ken Hislop, the Capital Projects Manager; and Andrew Hake, the Social Development Officer must receive special mention here. Events are proving that it is only with the help of officers like them, who have enthusiasm for new ideas and an understanding of the problems involved, that self-help groups can hope to gain the support they must have from local authorities.

[7] Department of the Environment Circular 118/75.

[8] The exclusion of women appears to be general amongst self-build groups. The reasons are not always clear, but generally I have found that the men seem to think that building is a man's job!

[9] Swindon Evening Advertiser Nov. 20 1974.

[10] Described in Chapter 15.

[11] Model Rules SH 1975 Published by the National Federation of Housing Associations

[12] Robert Clayton Alternative Building Design Group.

[13] Referred to in detail in Chapter 7.

[14] Shown in surveys carried out by the Department of the Environment, the National Federation of Housing Associations, and the Architectural Association.

[15] See Appendix A.

[16] In the western expansion of the town.

[17] See Appendix B.

[18] First report of the Working Party on the requirements for residential accommodation for single persons in the Borough of Thamesdown.
Housing Single People: 1. How they live at present

[19] Housing Single People: 2. A design guide with a description of a scheme at Leicester. Department of the Environment London HMSO 1974.

[20] The need for sponsorship is described in Chapters 9 and 16.

[21] As well as the Circular, the Guide Manual produced by SCD and the Handbook produced by the National Federation of Housing Associations provided valuable information for the formation of the Co-operative.

[22] Robert Clayton of Alternative Building Design Group.

[23] Set up in December 1976, its functions are described in Chapter 14. Its Director is John Hands, formerly Executive Director of SCD.

76

24 The formation of AHAS is described in Chapter 6.

25 Recently I was asked to give my views to a survey, carried out by one of the largest materials manufacturers and suppliers in this country, which was attempting to forecast the demands for building products in the next ten years. They were particularly interested to know what the potential demand was likely to be from the self-help sector.

26 This has the support of Governor Jerry Brown and the initial funding is now being considered by the Californian legislature.

27 The antecedents of such an advisory service go back a long way in time and geographical space: to John F. C. Turner's work in Peru with low income settlements where people made the most of limited resources by building dwellings for themselves; and to his consultancy monitoring and evaluation work in the late 1960's and early 1970's in the U.S.A. These all indicated user control to be a more economic way of providing satisfying housing for lower income groups prepared to work for it. The experience also showed that the right kind of 'professional' help and advice was necessary, particularly in the early stages, if such schemes were to be successful.

28 Bertha Turner had done important work in the U.S.A. in the 1960's on the evaluation of urban housing renewal and its effect on different ethnic groups in low income housing. This she had followed with field research for the U.S. Department of Housing and Urban Development resulting in the report "Owner-Built Housing in the U.S.A.". This experience, together with her knowledge of the British housing association and co-operative movement, was a valuable asset to the team.

Michael Drake had considerable experience of housing association administration and co-operative promotion, and had been a tenant in local authority public housing for 12 years. He represented his estate on the Association of London Housing Estates for many years, and at this time was Chairman of its Executive Committee. He gave evidence to the Government's Working Party on Housing Co-operatives, and was a founder-member of the National Federation of Co-operatives for which he wrote much of the draft constitution. His association with us was a natural outcome of the mutuality of our interests in more tenant control of public housing.

29 Section 12.

30 Published jointly by the Nationaly Federation of Housing Associations, the National Building Agency and the Housing Corporation first printed 1975, revised June 1978.

31 Published by the National Federation of Housing Associations in accordance with the Act.

32 The role of the Architect/Designer is dealt with in Chapter 11.

33 The role of the Managing Agencies is described in Chapter 15.

34 Income and corporation tax relief is available to approved societies under Section 341A of the Income and Corporation Taxes Act 1970 inserted into that Act by Section 120 of the Housing Act 1974.

35 Detailed guidance to these and other items of organisation are set out in the Manual referred to earlier.

36 Section 119 of the Act. This eligibility is preserved by Paragraph 13 of Schedule 5 of the Housing Rents and Subsidies Act 1975.

37 Section 9 (1) of the Housing Act 1974.

38 Under Section 3 (1) of the Act.

39 Under Section 4 of the Act.

40 Under Section 29 of the Act.

41 Section 26 (4A) of the Housing Subsidies Act 1967, inserted into that Act by Schedule 11 to the Housing Act 1974.

42 The Advisory Committee on Co-operatives, appointed by the Secretary of State for the Environment, has made a series of recommendations to the Government for

new legislation. But these significant changes in the law, intended to help housing co-operatives, will take a long time to come into effect. In the meantime existing legislation, designed for housing associations, is being used, as well as a Section inserted into the Housing Rents & Subsidies Act 1975.

[43] Final Report of the Working Party on Housing Co-operatives published by the Department of the Environment HMSO 1975.

[44] Resolution of the 23rd Congress of the International Co-operative Alliance held at Vienna from 5th to 8th September 1966.

[45] Bertha I. B. Turner has described most of the problems of co-operatives who rehabilitate existing urban property in her study "London Squatter Groups Becoming Housing Co-operatives", commissioned by the Building and Social Housing Foundation in 1977.

[46] Housing Corporation Circular 1/75.

[47] Even when a local authority provides the loan finance for building the scheme will still require the support of the Housing Corporation.

[48] In the case of the Toothill Co-operative this was for single people.

[49] Under the Industrial and Provident Societies Act 1965 in much the same way as the Self-Build Societies but with different rules.

[50] The role of the Co-operative Housing Agency is described in Chapter 14.

[51] The N.F.H.A. will take care of the registration of an affiliated co-operative, and provide a limited advisory service for an initial cost of £104 and an annual affiliation subscription of £18.

[52] The Model Rules are in accordance with the principles set out in 9.3.

[53] The example of Toothill Co-operative being an exceptional case with some hard lessons learned! (Chapter 5).

[54] Described in Chapter 16.

[55] These services have been set out in an excellent design manual for new build housing published by the Society for Co-operative Dwellings, a London-based Secondary Co-operative.

[56] CHA Directors' Report published in the Co-operative Housing Agency's newsletter CHAT March 1978.

[57] NFHA Co-operative Housing Handbook; and the CHA Outlines and their accompanying Handbooks.

[58] The statutory definition of a housing association is given in Section 189 of the Housing Act 1957 as amended by paragraph 6 of Schedule 13 Housing Act 1974.

[59] The criteria for registration is set out in the Housing Corporation's Practice notes for Housing Associations Appendix 1 (HAR 1/2) amd Memorandum HAR 1 (Co-op).

[60] Advice from the Local Authority is often helpful in this respect.

[61] Explained in the section on Finance.

[62] There are exceptions, but they are so few in number and untypical that it is considered to be misleading to quote them here.

[63] Under Section 119 of the Housing Act 1957 in the case of Local Authorities.

[64] It is out of these allowances that a sponsoring or servicing agency is paid.

[65] Under Section 32 of the Housing Act 1974. The terms of the grant are explained more simply in the Department of the Environment Circular 8/76.

[66] i.e. Where the rules restrict membership to tenants or prospective tenants and preclude the granting or assignment of tenancies to non-members, as is the case with the Model Rules.

[67] John F. C. Turner in the Book "Freedom to Build". Chapter 6 "The Re-Education of a Professional".

[68] Hans H. Harms in "Freedom to Build". Chapter 8. "User and Community involvement in Housing and its effects on Professionalism".

[69] Both the Architectural Association and the Department of the Environment surveys

of self-build in England and Wales found the building time taken with bricks and mortar construction was usually 18 months to 2 years.

70 "Self-Build Housing including the use of kits" Housing Development Directorate, January 1976. The report also recommended that the Directorate should resolve any possible problems with Building Regulations and Planning Controls.

71 (i) A manual for Self-Build Housing Associations: National Federation of Housing Associations.

(ii) New Build Design Manual for single people sharing: Society for Co-operative Dwellings.

72 Set up by the Housing Act 1964 to promote and assist the development of housing societies. Its functions were spelled out more specifically as regards self build societies in the Housing Act 1974.

73 Formed in December 1976 on the recommendations of the Working Party referred to in Chapter 9.

74 Appointed by the Secretary of State for the Environment

75 1978 CHA Directory of Housing Co-operatives

76 John Rouse in SCOOP 6, the newsletter of the Society for Co-operative Dwellings. This is a revealing account of his first Advisory Committee Meeting one of the first appointees to be chosen from a housing co-operative.

77 National Federation of Housing Association's Co-operative Housing Handbook, pp. 10—11.

78 According to the 1978 CHA Directory of Co-operatives there are now 3 secondaries registered with the Housing Corporation.

79 i.e. the acquisition and development allowances, and the management and maintenance allowances which are a part of the Housing Association Grant (see Chapter 10).

80 The Self-Build Manual is likely to deter many potential self-builders because of its emphasis on strict rules and regulations, and because it gives no indication of the possible short-cuts to speedy construction.

81 Whose address is Ladbroke House, Highbury Grove, London N5 2AD.

82 Many of their stories are told in the various publications listed in Appendix C.